M

Microsoft

Word 2013

FOR

DUMMIES

A Wiley Brand
POCKET EDITION

by Dan Gookin

JUL 0 1 2013

FOR

DUMMIES

A Wiley Brand

005,52
Word
Dummies

Microsoft® Word 2013 For Dummies® Pocket Edition

Published by
John Wiley & Sons, Inc.
111 River Street
Hoboken, NJ 07030-5774

www.wiley.com

Copyright © 2013 by John Wiley & Sons, Inc., Hoboken, New Jersey

Published simultaneously in Canada

For general information on our other products and services, please contact our Customer Care Department within the U.S. at 877-762-2974, outside the U.S. at 317-572-3993, or fax 317-572-4002.

For technical support, please visit www.wiley.com/techsupport.

Wiley also publishes its books in a variety of electronic formats. Some content that appears in print may not be available in electronic books.

Mini Edition ISBN-13: 978-1-118-53373-4 (pbk); ISBN: 978-1-118-56005-1 (ebk); ISBN: 978-1-118-55988-8 (ebk); ISBN: 978-1-118-55994-9 (ebk)

Manufactured in the United States of America

Publisher's Acknowledgments

We're proud of this book; please send us your comments through our online registration form located at `http://dummies.custhelp.com`.

Some of the people who helped bring this book to market include the following:

Acquisitions and Editorial

Senior Project Editor:
Mark Enochs

Senior Acquisitions Editor:
Katie Mohr

Copy Editor: Becky Whitney

Senior Editorial Manager:
Leah Michael

Cover Image: © tedestudio /
iStockphoto

Composition Services

Project Coordinator: Kristie Rees

Layout and Graphics:
Carrie A. Cesavice,
Jennifer Creasey

Proofreaders:
Lauren Mandelbaum,
Susan Moritz

Publishing and Editorial for Technology Dummies

> **Richard Swadley,** Vice President and Executive Group Publisher
>
> **Andy Cummings,** Vice President and Publisher
>
> **Mary Bednarek,** Executive Acquisitions Director
>
> **Mary C. Corder,** Editorial Director

Publishing for Consumer Dummies

> **Kathleen Nebenhaus,** Vice President and Executive Publisher

Composition Services

> **Debbie Stailey,** Director of Composition Services

Table of Contents

• •

Introduction

• •

T he only thing standing between you and your
writing is your word processor. Yeah, I know: It's
supposed to be helpful. Well, it tries. Computers can
do only so much. But you, as a smart person, are capable of so much more. I'm guessing that's why you
opened this book.

Welcome to *Word 2013 For Dummies,* Pocket Edition,
which removes the pain from using Microsoft's latest,
greatest, most confusing word processing software
ever! This book is your friendly, informative, and
entertaining guide to the routine of processing words
that is Word 2013.

Be warned: I'm not out to make you love Word. I don't
want you to enjoy the program. Use it, yes. Tolerate
it, of course. The only promise I'm offering is to ease
the pain that most people feel from using Microsoft
Word. Along the way, I kick Word in the butt, and I
hope you enjoy reading about it.

About This Book

I don't intend for you to read this book from cover to
cover. This book is a reference. Each chapter covers a
specific topic or task you can accomplish by using
Word 2013. Within a chapter, you find self-contained
sections, each of which describes how to perform a
specific task or get something done. Sample sections
you encounter in this book include

  ✔ Moving a block

  ✔ Check your spelling

> ✔ Save your stuff!
>
> ✔ How to format a paragraph

You hold in your hands an active book. The topics between this book's yellow-and-black covers are all geared toward getting things done in Word 2013. Because nothing is assumed, all you need to do is find the topic that interests you and read.

Word uses the mouse and keyboard to get things done. If your computer has a multi-touch monitor or you're using a tablet, you can touch the screen to get things done, though Word works best with a keyboard and mouse.

I use the word *click* to describe the action of clicking the mouse's main (left) button. Likewise, on a touchscreen, you can touch the screen rather than click with the mouse.

This is a keyboard shortcut: Ctrl+P

Simply press and hold the Ctrl (control) key and type the letter *P*, just as you would press Shift+P to create a capital *P*. When you're using the onscreen keyboard on a multi-touch monitor, keyboard shortcuts require two steps: First tap the Ctrl key, and then tap the P key, for example.

Sometimes, you must press more than two keys at the same time: Ctrl+Shift+T

In this line, you press Ctrl and Shift together and then press the T key. Release all three keys. (These key combinations are not possible when using the onscreen keyboard.)

Commands in Word 2013 exist as *command buttons* on the Ribbon interface. I may refer to the tab, the command group, and then the button itself to help you locate that command button — for example, the Page Color button in the Page Background group on the Design tab. Or I might write, "the Page Color button, found in the Design tab's Page Background group."

Menu commands are listed like this: Table⇨Insert Table

Choosing this command tells you to choose from the Table menu the command named Insert Table. The Table menu appears as a button on the Ribbon.

When I describe a message or something else you see onscreen, it looks like this:

```
Why should I bother to love
Evelyn when robots will
eventually destroy the human
race?
```

Icons Used in This Book

This icon flags useful, helpful tips or shortcuts.

This icon marks a friendly reminder to do something.

This icon marks a friendly reminder *not* to do something.

This icon alerts you to overly nerdy information and technical discussions of the topic at hand. The information is optional reading, but it may enhance your reputation at cocktail parties if you repeat it.

Where to Go from Here

Start reading! Observe the table of contents and find something that interests you. If you've been using a version of Word earlier than version 2007, you're probably somewhat surprised at the look of Word 2013. Therefore, I recommend that you start reading at Chapter 1.

Read! Write! Let your brilliance shine!

My e-mail address is dgookin@wambooli.com. Yes, that's my real address. I reply to all e-mail I receive, and you'll get a quick reply if you keep your question short and specific to this book or to Word itself. Although I enjoy saying "Hi," I cannot answer technical support questions or help you troubleshoot your computer. Thanks for understanding.

You can also visit my web page for more information or as a diversion:

www.wambooli.com

Enjoy this book. And enjoy Word. Or at least tolerate it.

Chapter 1

Hello, Word!

. . . .

In This Chapter

▶ Starting Word

▶ Deciphering the Word screen

▶ Quitting Word

▶ Minimizing Word

. . . .

*Y*ou can't do squat with a computer until you start the thing. Likewise, you can't even write the word *squat* until you start a word processing program. Because you bought *this* book and not *Pencils For Dummies,* the program you need to start is Microsoft Word. This chapter tells you how to get Word started and begin your word processing day. Let me also mention that reading this chapter is a far more enriching experience than reading *Pencils For Dummies,* which is barely a pamphlet, albeit one that's charmingly illustrated.

Get into Word

The Windows operating system is rife with various and sundry ways of getting things done. One victim of that variety is the way to start a program. Rather than bore you by listing all those ways, I figure that you simply want to know the best way to start Word. This section offers three solid choices.

- ✔ Before you can use Word, your computer must be on and toasty. Log in to Windows. Start your computer day. There's no need to put bread into your computer.

- ✔ Make sure that you're seated, with a nice, upright, firm posture as you write. They tell me that your wrists should be even with your elbows and that you shouldn't have to tilt your head forward. Shoulders are back and relaxed.

- ✔ Don't freak out because you're using a computer. You are in charge! Keep that in mind. Chant silently, over and over: "I am the master."

- ✔ If you need help starting your computer, refer to my book *PCs For Dummies* for quick and accurate turning-on-the-computer instructions.

- ✔ You can stop chanting "I am the master" now.

Starting Word the boring way

Without fail, the place to start any program in Windows is at the fabled Start button or, in Windows 8, on the Start screen.

In Windows 8, look for the Word 2013 tile on the Start screen. You may have to scroll the screen to the left to find the tile, as shown in the margin. Click or touch the tile to start the Word program.

In Windows 7, click the Start button, which is often found on the left side of the taskbar and at the bottom of the screen, adorned with the Windows logo. Choose Microsoft Word 2013 from the Start menu's list of programs.

What is a word processor?

At its core, a word processor is computer software —a program — that lets you create documents. That's really the key word — *documents*. A document includes formatted text, margins, maybe even a bit of artwork. The word processor contains all the tools to make that happen; this book explains how those tools work.

When Word isn't found on the Start menu's list of programs, choose the All Programs menu to look for it. Sometimes, it may be lurking on a Microsoft Office or Microsoft Office 2013 submenu.

After choosing the tile or icon to start Word, you can watch in amazement as the program unfurls its sails on your computer's monitor.

✔ Don't let Word's appearance overwhelm you! Later in this chapter, I describe what you're looking at, in the section "Examining Word's main screen."

✔ If you can't find Word's tile or icon, it may not be installed on your computer. This book is specific to Microsoft Word, not to the Microsoft Works word processor or any other word processor.

✔ I refer to the program as *Word,* though its icon may be labeled *Microsoft Word, Microsoft Office Word, Microsoft Word 2013,* or another variation.

Starting Word the best way

The *best* way to start Word, and the way I do it every day, is to pin the Word icon to the taskbar. That way, you can start Word directly from the Desktop.

In Windows 8, you can pin the icon to the taskbar by following these steps:

1. **Right-click the Word tile on the Start screen.**

2. **Choose the command Pin to Taskbar.**

   The Pin to Taskbar command is found at the bottom of the screen.

To confirm that the icon is properly pinned, press the Win+D keyboard shortcut to see the desktop.

In Windows 7, follow these steps to pin the Word icon to the taskbar:

1. **Find the Word icon on the Start button's All Programs menu.**

   Don't click the Word icon — just find it!

2. **Right-click the Word icon on the All Programs menu.**

3. **Choose the command Pin to Taskbar.**

   The Word icon is *pinned* (permanently added) to the taskbar.

To start Word, you merely click the Word icon that's placed on the taskbar. *Click!* And then Word starts. That's the fastest and bestest way to begin your word processing day.

Opening a document to start Word

You use the Word program to create *documents,* which are stored on your computer in much the same way as people pile junk into boxes and store them in their garages. But that's not important. What is important is that you can use those documents to start Word: Opening a Word document causes Word to start *and* to display that document for editing, printing, or giving others the impression that you're doing something.

What's your point, Dan?

My point is that you can also start Word by opening a Word document. Simply locate the Word document icon (shown in the margin) in a folder window. Double-click to open the document, and Word starts up on the screen, instantly (more or less) displaying the document for editing, reading, modifying, perusing, cussing, mangling, and potentially fouling up beyond all recognition.

✔ The Word document you open can be on the desktop, in the My Documents folder, or in any other folder or location where a Word document icon can lurk.

✔ The document name appears beneath or to the right of the icon. You can use the name to determine the document's contents — as long as the document was properly named when it was saved to disk. (More on that elsewhere in this book.)

You can see a Jump List of recently opened documents by right-clicking the Word icon on the taskbar. Choose a document from the list to start Word and open that document.

✔ Word is capable of opening other types of documents, including documents from previous versions of Word, Rich Text Format documents, and others. Each of these documents has its own icon, though the icon looks similar to the standard Word document icon.

Behold the Word Program

Like all programs in Windows, Word offers its visage in a program window. It's the place where you get your word processing work done.

Using the Word Start screen

The first thing you may see after starting Word is something called the Word Start screen, as shown in Figure 1-1. This screen appears only when you initially start Word and it works to help you get started by opening a recent document, browsing for a document file to open, or choosing a new type of document to start.

Choose a previous document.   Start a new blank document.

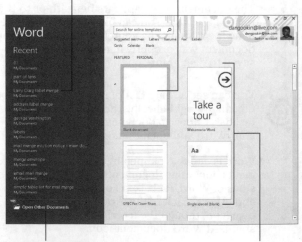

Browse for a document.   Select a template.

Figure 1-1: The Word Start screen.

Select an option, as illustrated in Figure 1-1, to get working. Or if you're waiting for your muse, choose the Blank Document item and you'll be on your way.

 If you're an old hand at Word, you probably desire to get rid of the Word Start screen. Follow these blessed steps:

1. **In Word, click the File tab on the Ribbon.**

   If you're still staring at the Word Start screen, choose the Blank Document item to get into Word. The File tab is the blue button that says *File,* found near the upper-left corner of the screen.

2. **Choose Options from the list of menu items on the left side of the screen.**

3. **Ensure that the General category is chosen from the left side of the Word Options window.**

4. **Remove the check mark by the item Show the Start Screen When This Application Starts.**

5. **Click the OK button.**

You can repeat these steps and restore the check mark in Step 4 if you want to resurrect the Word Start screen.

 The Word Start screen appears only when you first start Word. The Word Start screen doesn't appear if you start Word by opening a document. See the earlier section, "Opening a document to start Word."

Examining Word's main screen

It's the electronic version of a blank sheet of paper — and more. It's the *more* part that you might find daunting. The dee-dads and goo-bobs that surround the Word program window all have specific names that you need to know to get the most from the program. Figure 1-2 shows the big picture.

Figure 1-3 highlights the gizmos at the top of the Word window, showcasing the Ribbon interface.

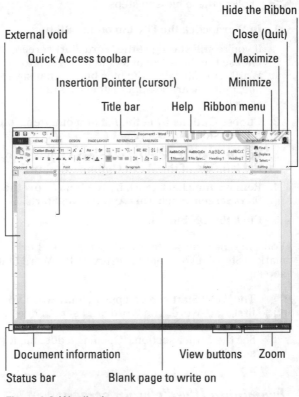

Hide the Ribbon

External void

Close (Quit)

Quick Access toolbar

Maximize

Insertion Pointer (cursor)

Minimize

Title bar   Help   Ribbon menu

Document information   View buttons   Zoom

Status bar   Blank page to write on

Figure 1-2: Word's visage.

File tab menu   Tabs   Command buttons

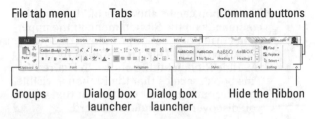

Groups   Dialog box   Dialog box   Hide the Ribbon
              launcher   launcher

Figure 1-3: The Ribbon.

 To get the most from Word's window, change the window size: As with any window, you can use the mouse to drag the window's edges in or out or click the window's Maximize button (the middle button in the window's upper-right corner) to have the window fill the screen.

✔ Word's window size affects what you see in the Ribbon command groups. When the Word window is smaller, fewer buttons show up, or they may show up in three rows. When the window is larger, you see more buttons, usually in two rows.

✔ The largest portion of Word's screen is for composing text. It's blank and white, just like a fresh sheet of paper. (Refer to Figure 1-2.) That's where you compose and format your text, and I cover that area specifically in the next section.

✔ The Ribbon contains all Word commands, which appear as buttons, input boxes, and menus. The Ribbon is divided into tabs (refer to Figure 1-3). The commands on the Ribbon are separated into groups. Some tabs may appear and disappear, depending on what you're doing in Word. And the commands in groups change as you change the window's size.

✔ The Ribbon can be shown or hidden by using commands on the Ribbon menu in the upper-right corner of the Word window (refer to Figure 1-2). You can also hide the Ribbon by clicking the Hide Ribbon button shown in Figure 1-3. This book assumes that the Ribbon is visible, and I recommend that you keep it that way as you discover the wonders of Word.

✔ The Windows taskbar, located at the bottom of the screen, is a part of Windows itself and not Word. However, as you open documents in Word, buttons representing those documents appear on the Windows taskbar.

 Clicking the File tab replaces the contents of the Word window with a screen full of commands and their descriptions. To return to the Word window, click the Back button (shown in the margin) or press the Esc key.

Working with Word on a tablet

If you're using Word on a tablet, you can adjust the spacing between buttons on the Ribbon by activating Touch mode. Follow these steps:

1. Click or touch the Customize Quick Access Toolbar button.

 The button is shown in the margin and found near the upper-left corner of the screen.

2. Choose Touch/Mouse Mode.

 The Touch/Mouse Mode button appears on the Quick Access toolbar, as shown in the margin.

3. Touch the Touch/Mouse Mode button and choose the command Touch.

The space between items on the Ribbon increases.

Hopefully, the extra space helps forgive how large your fingers are as you attempt to use Word on your mobile computing device or on a computer with a touchscreen monitor.

✔ Choose the Mouse command from the Touch/Mouse mode button to diminish (restore) the space between the buttons on the Ribbon.

✔ To remove the Touch Mode button, repeat Steps 1 and 2 in this section.

Writing in Word

Word's equivalent of the mind-numbing, writer's-block-inducing blank page can be found in the center part of the Word program window (refer to Figure 1-2). That's where the text you write, edit, and format appears. Unlike with a sheet of paper, however, the text you create in Word can be viewed in a number of different ways.

The most common way to view your document is to use Print Layout view, as shown in Figure 1-2. In this view, the entire page of text is displayed on the screen, looking just the way it prints. Print Layout view shows graphical images, columns, and all sorts of other fancy effects. You even see the blank space around pages, described as the ethereal void in the figure.

The other views are:

Read Mode: Use this mode to read a document like an eBook.

Web Layout: Use this mode when you undertake the dreadful possibility of using Word as a web page editor or to examine web pages you've saved.

Outline: This mode helps you organize your thoughts.

Draft: I prefer using Word in Draft view, which shows only basic text and not all the fancy features and formatting. Without that stuff on the screen, I can more easily concentrate on writing.

Switch between Read Mode, Print Layout, and Web Layout views by using the View buttons, found in the lower-right corner of the Word program window (refer to Figure 1-2). Clicking a button with the mouse changes the view.

To get to Outline and Draft views, click the Views tab and choose those views from the Views group.

Understanding the mouse pointer

Though word processing is a keyboard thing, you'll find that the computer mouse comes in handy. You use the mouse to choose commands, move around the document you're editing, and select text. This book explains all these topics elsewhere. For now, it helps to understand how the mouse pointer changes its look as you work in Word:

 For editing text, the mouse pointer becomes the I-beam.

 For choosing items, the standard 11 o'clock mouse pointer is used.

 For selecting lines of text, a 1 o'clock mouse pointer is used.

The mouse pointer may change its look when *click-and-type* mode is active: Lines appear to the left and right of, and below, the I-beam mouse pointer.

Cajoling Word to help you

Like most programs in Windows, a Help system is available in Word. You can summon it by pressing the F1 key, which displays the Word Help window. There you can type a topic, a command name, or even a question into the box to search for help.

The F1 key also works anytime you're deep in the bowels of Word and doing something specific. The Help information that's displayed tends to be specific to whatever you're doing in Word. Little buttons that look like question marks also summon Word Help.

 You can use the mouse to see what some of the little buttons and items with pictures on them do in Word. Just hover the mouse pointer over the button, and — voilà! — it's like Folgers instant information crystals.

End Your Word Processing Day

It's the pinnacle of etiquette to know when and how to excuse oneself. Leaving can be done well or poorly. For example, the phrase "Well, I must be off," works lots better than "Something more interesting must be happening somewhere else" — especially at Thanksgiving.

It's entirely possible to quit Word without hurting its feelings or bothering with etiquette. This section covers the many ways to end your word processing day.

Quitting Word

When you're done word processing and you don't expect to return to it anytime soon, you quit the Word program. Quitting a computer program is like putting away a book on a shelf. In the electronic world of the computer, you click the X button in the upper-right corner of the Word program window (refer to Figure 1-2).

The catch? You have to close each and every Word document window that's open before you can say that you've completely quit Word.

The other catch? Word won't quit during that shameful circumstance when you have unsaved documents. If so, you're prompted to save the document, as shown in Figure 1-4. My advice is to click the Save button to save your work.

Figure 1-4: Better click that Save button!

If you click the Don't Save button, your work isn't saved and Word quits. If you click the Cancel button, Word doesn't quit and you can continue working.

- ✔ See Chapter 7 for more information on saving documents.

- ✔ Also see Chapter 7 on how to recover drafts of documents you failed to save.

- ✔ You don't have to quit Word just to start editing another document. Refer to the next couple of sections for helpful, timesaving information!

✔ After quitting Word, you can continue to use Windows by starting up any other program, such as Spider Solitaire or perhaps something more calming, like *Call Of Duty*.

Closing a document without quitting Word

You don't always have to quit Word. For example, if you're merely stopping work on one document to work on another, quitting Word is a waste of time. Instead, you can *close* the document.

To close a document in Word, click the File tab and choose the Close command. Word banishes the document from its window, but then the program sits there and waits for you to do something else, such as start working on a new document or open a document you previously saved.

Bottom line: There's no point in quitting Word when all you want to do is start editing a new document.

✔ When you try to close a document before it has been saved, Word displays a warning dialog box (refer to Figure 1-4). Click the Save button to save your document. If you want to continue editing, click the Cancel button and get back to work.

✔ The keyboard shortcut for the Close command is Ctrl+W. This command may seem weird, but it's used to close documents in many programs.

Setting Word aside

There's no need to quit Word if you know that you will use it again soon. In fact, I've been known to keep Word open and running on my computer for *weeks* at a time. The secret is to use the Minimize button, found in the upper-right corner of the screen (refer to Figure 1-2).

Clicking the Minimize button shrinks the Word window to the taskbar, where it exists as a button. With the Word program window out of the way, you can do other things with your computer. Then when you're ready to word-process again, click the Word button on the taskbar to restore the Word window to the screen.

Chapter 2

The Typing Chapter

. . . .

In This Chapter

▶ Knowing the PC keyboard

▶ Typing on a touchscreen

▶ Using the spacebar

▶ Using the Enter key

▶ Observing the status bar

▶ Minding the space between pages

▶ Seeing stuff in your text that isn't there

▶ Living with weird underlines and colored text

. . . .

*W*ord processing is about using a keyboard. It's typing. That's the way computers were used for years, long before the mouse and all the fancy graphics became popular. Yep — ask a grizzled old-timer and you'll hear tales of ugly text screens and keyboard commands that would tie your fingers in knots. Though things aren't that bad today, I highly recommend that you bone up on your keyboard skills to get the most from your word processing duties. This chapter tells you what you need to know.

Behold the Keyboard!

Typing happens on a keyboard. At this point in the history of technology, the keyboard can be a physical keyboard or a touchscreen keyboard. This section explores the possibilities.

Using the PC keyboard

Though I'm sure you can easily recognize a computer keyboard, you should know how to refer to its various keys. To assist you, I illustrate a typical computer keyboard in Figure 2-1.

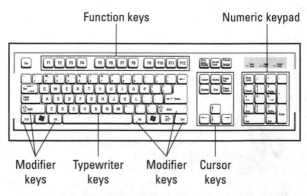

Figure 2-1: Famous attractions on the typical PC keyboard.

Generic terms are given to clusters of keys found on the PC keyboard. Know where the function keys are, the typewriter keys, cursor keys, and modifier keys, as illustrated in the figure.

Here are some individual keys worth noting:

✔ **Enter:** Marked with the word *Enter* and sometimes a cryptic, bent-arrow thing, this key is
used to end a paragraph of text. See the later
section, "Pressing the Enter key."

✔ **Spacebar:** The only key with no symbol, it
inserts spaces between words. Only one space!
See the later section, "Whacking the spacebar."

✔ **Tab:** This key inserts the tab "character," which
shoves the next text you type over to the next
tab stop. It's an interesting and potentially frus-
trating formatting key.

✔ **Backspace and Delete:** These keys are used to
back up and erase text, which is a function
many writers find handy. Read more about
these keys in Chapter 4.

Every character key you press on the keyboard pro-
duces a character on the screen, on the blank part
where you write. Typing those character keys over
and over is how you write text on a word processor.

✔ The **Shift** key is used to produce capital letters;
otherwise, the text you type is in lowercase.

✔ Keys on the **numeric keypad** serve sometimes
as cursor keys and sometimes as number keys.
The split personality is evident on each key cap,
which displays two symbols. The **Num Lock** key
and its corresponding light are on if the numeric
keypad (1, 2, 3) is active. If the cursor keys
(arrows, Home) are active, Num Lock is off.

✔ **Cursor keys** are also called *arrow keys;* they
control the cursor. Also included are the non-
arrow keys: Home, End, PgUp (or Page Up),
PgDn (or Page Down), Insert, and Delete.

✔ **Ctrl** is pronounced "control." The variety of
names that people give to the Ctrl key before
they know it as *the control key* is amazing.

> ✔ The **Delete** key may also be labeled Del on your keyboard.
>
> ✔ **Modifier keys** do nothing by themselves. Instead, the Shift, Ctrl, and Alt keys work in combination with other keys.

 The **Caps Lock** key lets you type text in UPPER CASE letters. After you press Caps Lock, the Caps Lock light on your keyboard comes on, indicating that you're entering ALL CAPS mode. Press the Caps Lock key again to return to normal.

Working a touchscreen keyboard

It's possible, and I'm not thrilled about it, but you can use Word 2013 in an environment where you type on the monitor, not on a keyboard. In this case, typing takes place on a virtual keyboard, similar to the one shown in Figure 2-2.

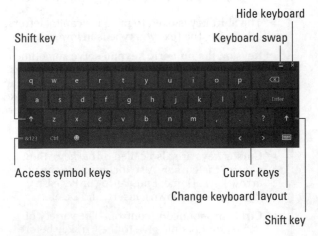

Figure 2-2: A tablet's onscreen keyboard.

The onscreen keyboard's operation works basically the same as a real keyboard: You type text with your fingers, albeit probably not as fast as on a physical keyboard. Accessing some of the specialized keys (function keys, cursor keys, and so on) is problematic. Still, the idea of using Word on a touchscreen seems to be more of a quick-and-dirty thing than something you would seriously spend time doing.

Then again, I don't know how tolerant you are for pain.

✔ Using the Ctrl key on the onscreen keyboard is a two-step process: Touch the Ctrl key and then touch another key.

✔ Not all Ctrl-key combinations in Word can be produced by using the onscreen keyboard.

✔ Refer to Chapter 1 for information on activating Touch mode, which makes it easier to use Word on a tablet.

You need a computer to create a document. It's possible to edit a document, or even create small documents, using a tablet, but it's not the best tool for a job.

The Old Hunt-and-Peck

After starting Word, you'll most likely type these words next: *Clackity-clack-clack-clack.*

Or on a tablet: *Smudge-smear-poke-poke-poke.*

The text you type on the keyboard appears on the screen — even the typos and mistakes and bad grammar: It all falls into place regardless of your intent, posture, or good looks. This section offers some basic typing tips, suggestions, and advice.

Following the cursor

The key to writing in Word is to look for the *insertion pointer* in your text. It's a flashing vertical bar:

On a touchscreen, the vertical bar occasionally grows a circle, like an upside-down lollipop:

Use the circle to help move the cursor around; refer to Chapter 3.

Text you type appears *before* the insertion pointer, one character at a time. After a character appears, the insertion pointer hops to the right, making room for more text. For example, type this line:

```
I want a helping of beets!
```

The insertion pointer moves to the right, marching along as you type. It's called an *insertion* pointer for a reason: Press the left-arrow key a few times to move the insertion pointer back before the word *helping*.

Type the word *second* and a space. The word (and the space) is inserted into your text. The text to the right is pushed off to make room for the new text. Now the sentence should read:

```
I want a second helping of beets!
```

Chapter 3 covers moving the insertion pointer around in more detail.

When using a multi-touch monitor and the onscreen keyboard, you may occasionally see word suggestions appear as you type. Touch the suggestion to have that word automatically inserted into the text.

Whacking the spacebar

Pressing the spacebar inserts a *space character* into the text. Spaces are important between words and sentences. Withoutthemreadingwouldbedifficult.

The most important thing to remember about the spacebar is that you need to whack it only once. In word processing, as in all typing done on a computer, only *one* space appears between words and after punctuation. That's it!

✔ I'm serious! If you're an old-timer, you're probably used to putting two spaces after a period, which is what they once taught in typing class, back in the last century. This extra space is wrong on a computer; typing it doesn't add more room between words or sentences in a word processor. Trust me on that.

✔ Anytime you feel like using two or more spaces, what you need is a tab. Tabs are best for indenting text as well as for lining up text in columns.

The reason that only one space is needed between sentences is that computers use proportionally spaced type. Old-fashioned typewriters used monospace type, so pressing the spacebar twice after a sentence was supposed to aid in readability (though it's debatable). Computer type is more like professionally typeset material, and both typesetters and professional-document folks know to put only one space after a period or a colon.

If you want to type two spaces after a period and actually see them, choose a monospace font, such as Courier.

Backing up and erasing

When you make a typo or another type of typing error, press the Backspace key on the keyboard. The Backspace key is used to back up and erase. The Delete key can also be used to erase text, though it gobbles up characters to the *right* of the insertion pointer. See Chapter 4 for more information on deleting text.

Pressing the Enter key

In word processing, you press the Enter key only when you reach the end of a paragraph. Though pressing Enter at the end of a line of text might seem logical, there's no need: Word takes the text that hangs over the end of a line and wraps it down to the next line. Therefore, you press Enter only to end a paragraph.

To practice pressing the Enter key at the end of a paragraph, type the following text:

```
Cindy was very convincing. She explained
to her 4-year-old brother that snails
were a delicacy in France, so the moist,
slow-moving monopods were completely
safe. Yet Zach was dubious. Sure, he
loved his big sister. And while he
didn't mind occasionally popping a
snail's delicate shell between his toes,
he most definitely wasn't going to put
one in his mouth.
```

Now that you're done typing the paragraph, press the Enter key. There. You did it right.

> ✔ There's no need to use the Enter key when you want to double-space your text. Double-spacing uses a text formatting command in Word. See Chapter 6 for more about formatting.

> ✔ Neither do you need to press the Enter key twice to add extra space between your paragraphs. Word can automatically add space before or after paragraphs.

> ✔ If you want to indent a paragraph, press the Tab key after pressing Enter. This can also be done automatically; refer again to Chapter 6.

 The process of taking text from the end of one line and placing it at the start of the next line is named *word wrap*.

Curse you, Sticky Keys!

As your mind wanders, your fingers absently press and release the Shift key. Suddenly, you see the warning: Sticky Keys! By pressing the Shift, Ctrl, or Alt key five times in a row, you activate the Windows Sticky Keys function, a tool designed to make a computer keyboard more accessible to people. If you don't need the help, you'll probably find the intrusion annoying.

Don't panic! You can easily turn off the Sticky Keys feature: In the Sticky Keys warning dialog box, click the link titled Go to the Ease of Access Center to Disable the Keyboard Shortcut. In the dialog box that appears, remove the check marks by any and all Sticky Keys options and settings. Click OK and you'll never be bothered again!

Stuff That Happens While You Type

As you madly compose your text, fingers energetically jabbing the buttons on the keyboard, you may notice a few things happening on the screen. You might see spots. You might see lines and boxes. You may even see lightning! All are side effects of typing in Word. They're normal, and they're explained in this section.

Watching the status bar

The reason it's the *status* bar is that it can show you the status of your document, updating information as you type, as shown in Figure 2-3.

Current page

Word count   Other stuff may appear here.

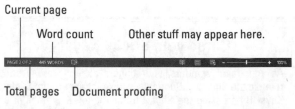

Total pages   Document proofing

Figure 2-3: Stuff that lurks on the status bar.

The type of information that's displayed, as well as how much information is displayed, depends on how you configure Word.

To better view the status bar when typing with the onscreen keyboard, touch the Keyboard Swap button, shown in the margin. After you touch the button, the status bar jumps up, above the keyboard.

Observing page breaks

Word tries its best to show you where one page ends and another page begins. This feature is most helpful because oftentimes you want to keep elements on one page, or maybe folks just like to know when the text they're writing flows from one page to the next.

The status bar helps you discover which page you're working on. For example, the page-number indicator changes from 6 to 7 when you start a new page. Word also shows you graphically where one page ends and another begins.

In Print Layout view, which is the way Word normally shows your document, you see virtual pages and a space between them, as shown in Figure 2-4.

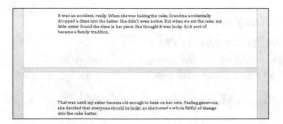

It was an accident, really. When she was baking the cake, Grandma accidentally dropped a dime into the batter. She didn't even notice. But when we ate the cake, my little sister found the dime in her piece. She thought it was lucky. So it sort of became a family tradition.

That was until my sister became old enough to bake on her own. Feeling generous, she decided that everyone should be lucky, so she tossed a whole fistful of change into the cake batter.

Figure 2-4: The page break in Print Layout view.

Text appearing above the ethereal void is on one page, and text below the void is on the next page. Yes, it looks just like real sheets of paper.

In Word, only the Print Layout and Draft views show page breaks. In Draft view, the page break appears as a line of dots marching across the screen. Refer to Chapter 1 for more information on Print Layout and Draft views.

You can change the gap between pages in Print Layout view. Point the mouse at the gap. When the mouse pointer changes, as shown in the margin, double-click to either close or open the gap.

My advice: Don't force a page break by pressing the Enter key a gazillion times. You'll regret it.

Working collapsible headers

You may see a tiny triangle to the left of various headings in your documents. These triangles allow you to expand or collapse all text in the header's section. Click once to collapse the text; click again to expand it.

Dealing with spots and clutter in the text

There's no cause for alarm if you see spots — or dots — amid the text you type, such as

```
This·can·be·very·annoying.¶
```

What you're seeing are *nonprinting characters*. Word uses various symbols to represent things you normally don't see: spaces, tabs, the Enter key, and more.

To turn these items on or off, click the Show/ Hide button on the Home tab in the Paragraph group. Click once to show the goobers; click again to hide them. The keyboard shortcut for the Show/Hide command is Ctrl+Shift+8.

Why bother with showing the goobers? Sometimes, it's useful to check out what's up with formatting, find stray tabs visually, or locate missing paragraphs, for example. (*WordPerfect users:* It's as close as you can get in Word to the Reveal Codes command.)

Understanding colored underlines

Adding underlining to your text in Word is cinchy; Chapter 6 tells you all about character format. Yet sometimes Word may do some underlining and add strange-colored text on its own.

Red zigzag: Spelling errors in Word are underlined with red zigzags. See Chapter 5.

Blue zigzag: Grammatical and word-choice errors are flagged with a special blue zigzag. The blue underlined text is most likely not the best choice for you to use.

Blue underlines: Word courteously highlights web page addresses by using blue, underlined text in your document. You can Ctrl+click the blue underlined text to visit the web page.

Red lines: You may see red lines in the margin, underneath or through text. If so, it means that you're using Word's Track Changes feature.

Chapter 3

Moving To and Fro and Blocking Text

● ●

In This Chapter
▶ Using the scroll bars
▶ Moving the insertion pointer
▶ Getting around with keyboard shortcuts
▶ Getting lost and getting back
▶ Using the Go To command
▶ Marking blocks of text
▶ Unblocking text
▶ Copying, moving, and pasting blocks of text

● ●

1 like the word *fro.* I like the word *yon.* They're archaic in the English language, referring to a direction and a location, respectively. *Fro* makes no sense by itself, so it's used in the phrase *to and fro,* which refers to going somewhere and then back again. *Yon* is often seen with its friends *hither* and *thither,* meaning "here" and "there."

As you work in Word, you find yourself moving to and fro and hither, thither, and yon. That's because writing text isn't always a linear task. You need to move that little insertion-pointer guy around the document. It's basic movement, and it's one topic of this chapter.

Working with text blocks is the other topic, and you'll find plenty of interesting blocks when it comes to writing. First are those moveable blocks used by the ancient Chinese for printing. Then comes the inevitable writer's block. In Word, you can take advantage of blocks of text in a document, which is probably far more useful than the other types of blocks. That's because working with blocks in Word is like playing with blocks as a kid: Mix in some, cut, copy, and paste, and you have this engaging chapter on working with blocks of text.

Scroll Through a Document

It's ironic that the word *scroll* is used to refer to an electronic document. The scroll was the first form of portable recorded text, existing long before bound books. On a computer, scrolling is the process by which you view a little bit of a big document in a tiny window. This section explains how scrolling is relevant in Word.

Using the vertical scroll bar

On the right side of the Word program window, you find the vertical scroll bar, illustrated in Figure 3-1. The bar can disappear at times; move the mouse over your text, and it shows up again.

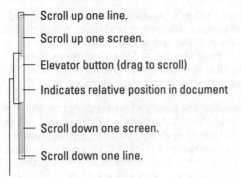

Scroll up one line.

Scroll up one screen.

Elevator button (drag to scroll)

Indicates relative position in document

Scroll down one screen.

Scroll down one line.

Portion of document on screen

Figure 3-1: The vertical scroll bar.

The vertical scroll bar's operation is similar to the scroll bar in any Windows program:

  ✔ Click the up- or down-arrow buttons at the top and bottom of the vertical scroll bar to scroll your document up or down. The document scrolls one line of text for each time you click those up- or down-arrow buttons.

  ✔ An *elevator button* appears inside the scroll bar. You can drag this button with the mouse, up or down, to scroll the document.

  ✔ You can click above or below the elevator button to scroll up or down one screen of text at a time.

The elevator button's size reflects how much of your document you can see at a time. When the button doesn't show up, or is dimmed, the whole document appears onscreen. Otherwise, the elevator button becomes smaller as your document grows longer.

The elevator button's position also helps show you which part of your document is visible. When the elevator button is at the top of the scroll bar, you're viewing text near the start of the document. When the elevator button is toward the bottom of the scroll bar, you're seeing text near the document's end.

Special bonuses are involved when you drag the elevator button to scroll through your document. As you drag the button up or down, you see a page number displayed, as shown in Figure 3-2. When a document is formatted with heading styles, you also see the heading title below the page number.

Figure 3-2: Scroll bar page-number info.

Scrolling through your document doesn't move the insertion pointer. If you start typing, don't be surprised when Word jumps back to where the insertion pointer lurks.

Using the horizontal scroll bar

The horizontal scroll bar appears just above the status bar, at the bottom of the Word window — but only when your document is wider than the window. When that happens, you can use the horizontal scroll bar to shift the page back and forth, left and right.

When the horizontal (left-right) shifting bugs you, consider using Word's Zoom tool to adjust the size of your document on the screen.

Scrolling with a mouse or finger

Aside from manipulating the scroll bars, you can use your computer mouse to scurry and scamper about your document. Sadly, this suggestion works only when you have one of those wheel mice. Coincidentally, you do all these tricks by manipulating that unique wheel button:

✔ Roll the wheel up or down to scroll your document up or down.

✔ Press and hold the wheel button to activate scrolling mode. With the wheel button down, you can move the mouse up or down to *pan* your document in that direction.

✔ If the mouse's wheel button also tilts from side to side, you can use it to pan left and right.

For computers and tablets with a touchscreen, scroll your document by using your finger: Swipe the screen up to scroll down; swipe the screen down to scroll up. Don't worry! It makes sense when you do it.

Move the Insertion Pointer

The beauty of the word processor is that you can edit any part of your document; you don't always have to work at "the end." The key to pulling off this trick is to know how to move the insertion pointer to the exact spot you want.

Commanding the insertion pointer

The easiest way to put the insertion pointer exactly where you want it is to point the mouse at that spot in your text and then click the mouse button. Point, click, move insertion pointer. Simple.

If you have a touchscreen monitor or are using a tablet, you can move the insertion pointer to any specific location by touching the text with your finger. Use the circle that appears below the insertion pointer for precise positioning.

Moving with the arrow keys

For short hops, nothing beats using the keyboard's arrow keys to quickly move the insertion pointer around a document. The four basic arrow keys move the insertion pointer up, down, right, and left:

Press This Key	*To Move the Insertion Pointer*
↑	Up to the preceding line of text
↓	Down to the next line of text
→	Right to the next character
←	Left to the preceding character

Moving the cursor doesn't erase characters. See Chapter 4 for information on deleting stuff.

If you press and hold the Ctrl (Control) key and then press an arrow key, you enter Jump mode. The invigorated insertion pointer leaps desperately in all four directions:

Press This Key Combo	*To Move the Insertion Pointer*
Ctrl+↑	Up to the start of the previous paragraph
Ctrl+↓	Down to the start of the next paragraph
Ctrl+→	Right to the start (first letter) of the next word
Ctrl+←	Left to the start (first letter) of the previous word

Moving from beginning to end

The insertion pointer also bows to pressure from those cursor keys without arrows on them. The first couple consists of End and Home, which move the insertion pointer to the start or end of something, depending on how End and Home are used:

Press This Key or Combination	To Whisk the Insertion Pointer
End	To the end of a line of text
Home	To the start of a line of text
Ctrl+End	To the end of the document
Ctrl+Home	To the tippy-top of the document

The remaining cursor keys are the Page Up or PgUp key and the Page Down or PgDn key. As you might guess, using these keys doesn't move up or down a page in your document. Nope. Instead, they slide through your document one screen at a time. Here's the roundup:

Press This Key or Combination	To Whisk the Insertion Pointer
PgUp	Up one screen or to the tippy-top of your document, if you happen to be near it
PgDn	Down one screen or to the end of the document, if you happen to be near it
Ctrl+Alt+PgUp	To the top of the current screen
Ctrl+Alt+PgDn	To the bottom of the current screen

The key combinations to move to the top or bottom of the current screen are Ctrl+Alt+PgUp and Ctrl+Alt+PgDn. That's Ctrl+Alt, not just the Ctrl key. And yes, few people use these commands.

You may be tempted to use Ctrl+PgUp and Ctrl+PgDn, but don't: These keyboard shortcuts work with the Find command. See Chapter 5.

Go Back to Where You Once Edited

Considering all the various commands for moving the insertion pointer, it's quite possible to make a mistake and not know where you are in a document. Yea, verily, the insertion pointer has gone where no insertion pointer has gone before.

Rather than click your heels together three times and try to get back the wishful way, just remember this keyboard combination: **Shift+F5.**

Pressing the Shift+F5 keys forces Word to return you to the last spot you edited. You can do this as many as three times before the cycle repeats. But the first time should get you back to where you were before you got lost.

Go to Wherever with the Go To Command

Word's Go To command allows you to send the insertion pointer to a specific page or line or to the location of a number of interesting elements that Word can potentially cram into your document. The Go To command is your word processing teleporter to anywhere.

To use the Go To command, click the Find button in the Home tab's editing group. Choose the Go To command from the menu. Or you can use the Ctrl+G keyboard shortcut. Either way, the Go To tab portion of the Find and Replace dialog box appears, as shown in Figure 3-3.

Figure 3-3: Telling Word to Go To you-know-where.

Choose which element to go to, such as a page, from the scrolling list on the left side of the dialog box. Then type the relevant information, such as a page number, in the box on the right side of the dialog box. Click the Go To button to go to that location. For example, type **14** in the box and press Enter, and you go to page 14 — if you have a page 14 to go to.

Note that you can go to a page *relative* to the current page. For example, to go three pages forward, choose Page and type **+3**. To go 12 pages backward, type **-12** in the box.

The Tao of Text Blocks

A *block* is simply a portion of text in your document, from a single character to the entire document. The block has a beginning and an end, and the block itself consists of all the text between them. You create a block by selecting text. You *select* text by using the keyboard or the mouse or one of various other text-selection techniques covered in this chapter.

On the screen, the block appears highlighted, as shown in Figure 3-4.

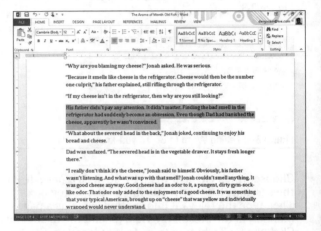

Figure 3-4: A block of text is selected.

By marking off text as a block, you can perform certain actions, or use various Word commands, that affect only the text in that block. Or you can copy, move, or delete the block of text.

- ✔ A block of text in Word includes all letters and characters *and* the text formatting.
- ✔ Graphics and other nontext elements can also be selected as a block. In fact, you can select graphics along with text in the same block.

✔ When the status bar is displaying a word count, the number of words selected in the block of text is displayed, next to the total number of words in the document. (Refer to Figure 3-4.)

✔ When the Find command locates text, the text is selected as a block. Refer to Chapter 5 for more information on the Find command.

Select Text with the Keyboard

The secret to using the keyboard to select text is the Shift key. By holding down the Shift key, you can use the standard keyboard commands that move the insertion pointer to select blocks of text. The following table has some suggestions for you.

To Select This	*Press This*
A character at a time to the right of the insertion pointer	Shift+→
A character at a time to the left of the insertion pointer	Shift+←
A block of text from the insertion pointer to the end of the line	Shift+End
A block of text from the insertion pointer to the beginning of the line	Shift+Home
A block of text from the insertion pointer to a line above	Shift+↑
A block of text from the insertion pointer to a line below	Shift+↓

You can use any keyboard cursor-movement command (I list them in prior sections), but I recommend using this Shift key method for selecting only small chunks of text. Otherwise, you may end up tying your fingers into knots!

Select Text on a Touchscreen

It's cinchy to mark a block of text on a multi-touch monitor: Simply drag your finger over the text. Because this procedure may also scroll the document, a better option is to *long-press* a word.

To do so, touch and hold the screen to select a single word. The word becomes selected, but also grows two lollipop insertion pointers on each end. You can then drag each of the insertion pointers to extend the selection.

To work with a selected block on a touchscreen, touch the block. You see the touchscreen version of the Mini toolbar, shown in Figure 3-5. The commands on that toolbar help manipulate the block.

Block commands   Mini toolbar commands   Menu

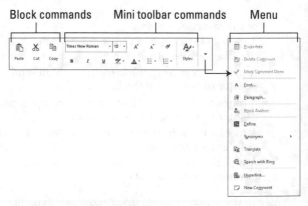

Figure 3-5: Touchscreen toolbar.

Mark a Block with the Mouse

Forget cheese. The computer mouse was born to mark text, by selecting vast swaths of words with a wide sweep of your hand, by clicking a number of times, or by using the old click-and-drag routine. Mickey may rule a kingdom, but your computer mouse rules over text selection in your computer.

Drag over text to select it

The most common way to select text is by using the computer mouse. Point the mouse at the start of the text block, and then drag the mouse over the text you want to select. As you drag, the text becomes highlighted or selected. (Refer to Figure 3-4.) Release the mouse — stop the dragging — to mark the end of the block.

 You can use this simple technique to select any old block size in your document, though it works best when you use the mouse to drag over only the text you can see on the screen. When you try to select text beyond what you see on the screen, you have to select and scroll — which can be unwieldy; the mouse scrolls the text up and down quickly and, well, things get out of hand.

When you find yourself becoming frustrated over not selecting all or part of a word, you can work with Word to put an end to the nonsense. When you're selecting more than a single word, the mouse tends to grab text a full word at a time. If you want Word to select text by characters rather than by words (which is what I prefer), follow these steps:

1. **Choose the Options command from the File tab's menu.**

2. **Choose Advanced from the list on the left side of the Word Options window.**

3. **Under the Editing Options heading, remove the check mark by the item labeled When Selecting Automatically Select Entire Word.**

4. **Click OK.**

Click the mouse to select text

A speedy way to select specific sizes of chunks of text is to match the power of the mouse with the dexterity of your index finger. The following table explains some clicking-and-selecting techniques worth noting.

To Select This Chunk of Text	*Click the Mouse Thusly*
A single word	Point at the word with your mouse and double-click.
A line	Move the mouse pointer into the left margin beside the line you want to select. The mouse pointer changes to an arrow pointing northeastward. Click the mouse to select a line of text, or drag the mouse up or down to select several lines.
A sentence	Position the insertion pointer over the sentence and Ctrl+click. (Press the Ctrl key and click the mouse.)
A paragraph	Point the mouse somewhere in the paragraph's midst and triple-click.

Select text with the old poke-and-point

 Here's the best way to select a chunk of text of any size, especially when that chunk of text is larger than what you can see on the screen at one time:

1. **Click the mouse to set the insertion pointer wherever you want the block to start — the anchor point.**

2. **Scroll through your document.**

   You must use the scroll bar or the mouse wheel to scroll through your document. If you use the cursor-movement keys, you reposition the insertion pointer, which isn't what you want.

3. **To mark the end of the block, press and hold the Shift key and click the mouse where you want the block to end.**

   The text from the insertion pointer to wherever you clicked the mouse is selected as a block.

Using the F8 Key to Mark a Block

Yes, wacky as it sounds, the F8 key is used to mark a block of text. Pressing F8 once enters *Extended Selection* mode. That's where Word drops anchor at the insertion pointer's location, and then lets you use either the mouse or the cursor keys to select text. In fact, you cannot do anything but select text in Extended Selection mode.

As an example, follow these steps to use the F8 key to mark a block of text:

1. **Position the insertion pointer at the start of the block of text.**

2. **Press the F8 key to drop anchor and mark one end of the block.**

3. **Use the keyboard's cursor keys to select the block of text.**

 Press a letter key to select text up to and including that letter. If you press N, you select all text up to and including the next *N* in your document. Nice. Nifty. Neat-o.

Word highlights text from the point where you dropped anchor with F8 to wherever you move the insertion pointer.

4. **Do something with the selected block of text.**

Word remains in Extended Selection mode until you do something with the block or you press the Esc key to cancel Extended Selection mode.

Doing something with a block of text is covered in the section "Manipulate the Block of Text" later in this chapter.

 Press the F8 key twice to select the current word (the one the insertion pointer is blinking inside of). Press the F8 key thrice (three times) to select the current sentence. Press the F8 key four times to select the current paragraph as a block of text. Press the F8 key five times to select the entire document, from top to bottom.

 No matter how many times you press F8, be aware that it always drops anchor. So pressing F8 once or five times means that Word is still in Extended Selection mode. Do something with the block or press Esc to cancel that mode. When you press the Esc key, you cancel the mode but keep the block of text marked.

Blocking the Whole Dang-Doodle Document

The biggest block you can mark is an entire document. Word has a specific command to do it, to select all text in a document: From the Home tab, locate the Editing area. (Click the Editing button when the entire Editing area isn't visible.) Then choose Select⇨Select All. Instantly, the entire document is marked as a single block o' text.

From the keyboard, you can use Ctrl+A to select an entire document or press the F8 key five times. Or you can even use the obscure Ctrl+5 (the 5 on the numeric keypad) key combo.

Deselecting a Block

When you mark a block of text and change your mind, you must unmark, or *deselect,* the text. Here are a few handy ways to do it:

✔ **Move the insertion pointer.** It doesn't matter how you move the insertion pointer, with the keyboard or with the mouse — doing so unhighlights the block. Note that this trick doesn't exit the F8 key's Extended Selection mode.

✔ **Press the Esc key and then the ← key.** This method works to end Extended Selection mode.

✔ **Press Shift+F5.** The Shift+F5 key combo is the "go back" command, but it also deselects a block of text *and* returns you to the text you were editing before making the selection.

Manipulate the Block of Text

What can you do with those marked blocks of text? Why, plenty of things! You can apply a format to all text in the block, copy a block, move a block, search through a block, proof a block, print a block, and even delete a block. The information in this section explains those tricks.

Blocks must be selected before you can manipulate them. When a block of text is marked, various Word commands affect only the text in that block.

✔ To replace a block, type some text. The new text (actually, the initial character) replaces the entire block.

✔ Delete a block by pressing the Delete or Backspace key. Thwoop! The block is gone.

✔ Formatting commands can be applied to any marked block of text — specifically, character and paragraph formatting. See Chapter 6 of this book.

Copying a block

After a block is marked, you can copy it into another part of your document to duplicate the text. The original block remains untouched by this operation. Follow these steps:

1. **Mark the block.**

   Detailed instructions about doing this task are offered in the first part of this chapter.

2. **From the Home tab, choose the Copy tool from the Clipboard group or press Ctrl+C on your keyboard.**

You get no visual clue that the text has been copied; it remains selected.

3. **Move the insertion pointer to the position where you want to place the block's copy.**

4. **Choose the Paste tool from the Clipboard area or press Ctrl+V on your keyboard.**

The block of text you copy is inserted into your text just as though you had typed it there by yourself.

After you copy a block, you can paste it into your document a second time. That's because whenever a block of text is cut or copied, Word remembers it. You use Ctrl+V, the Paste shortcut. Pasting text again simply pastes down a second copy of the block, spit-spot (as Mary Poppins would say).

Moving a block

To move a block of text, you select the text and then *cut* and paste. This process is almost exactly the same as copying a block, described in the preceding section, although in Step 2 you choose the Cut tool rather than the Copy tool or press the Ctrl+X keyboard shortcut for the Cut command. Otherwise, all steps are the same.

Don't be alarmed when the block of text vanishes! That's cutting in action; the block of text is being *moved,* not copied. You see the block of text again when you paste it in place. If you screw up, the Ctrl+Z Undo shortcut undoes a block move.

Setting the pasted text format

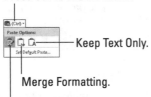

When you paste text in Word, the Paste Options icon appears near the pasted block of text, as shown in the margin. Don't let it annoy you! That button allows you to select formatting for the pasted block because occasionally the block may contain formatting that, well, looks quite ugly after it's pasted in.

To work the Paste Options button, click it with the mouse or press and release the Ctrl key on the keyboard. You see a menu of options, illustrated in Figure 3-6.

Press Ctrl to see the menu.

—————— Keep Text Only.

Merge Formatting.

Keep Source Formatting.

Figure 3-6: Pasting options.

Using the Paste Options icon is utterly optional. In fact, you can continue typing or working in Word and the icon bows out, fading away like some nebbish who boldly asked a power blonde to go out with him and she utterly failed to recognize his existence. Like that.

Copying or moving a block with the mouse

When you have to move a block only a short distance, you can use the mouse to drag-move or drag-copy the block. This feature works best when you're moving or copying a block to a location that you can see right on the screen. Otherwise, you're scrolling your document with the mouse while you're playing with blocks, which is like trying to grab an angry snake.

To move any selected block of text with the mouse, just drag the block: Point the mouse cursor anywhere in the blocked text, and then drag the block to its new location. Notice how the mouse pointer changes, as shown in the margin. That means you're moving the block of text.

Copying a block with the mouse works just like moving the block, except that you press the Ctrl key as you drag. When you do that, a plus sign appears in the mouse pointer (see the margin). It's your sign that the block is being copied and not just moved.

When you drag a block of text with the mouse, you're not copying it to the Clipboard. You cannot use the Paste (Ctrl+V) command to paste in the block again.

Chapter 4

Text Editing

● ●

In This Chapter

▶ Deleting characters, lines, sentences, paragraphs, and pages

▶ Splitting and joining paragraphs

▶ Dealing with returns

▶ Undoing your mistakes

▶ Using the Redo (Undo-Undo) command

● ●

1 believe that writing involves two parts of your brain: The wild, creative-burst part is the typing part. Then there's the tame, controlled-editing part. You need both parts in order to write anything good. In fact, I'd wager that people who become frustrated with writing are too quick to enter the controlled-editing part. Don't fall into that trap: Write! Spew forth your words! Editing your text is easier when you have lots of words than when you have only a scant few.

When you're ready to edit, you'll use Word's text editing commands. They all basically delete the stuff you've written. That's right: Editing text is basically the same task as ruthlessly slashing away words from your text. Word comes with ample tools to make that happen. Use them freely, as described in this chapter. But get your abundance of words down on paper before you enter the vicious slashing mode.

Remove Text You Don't Want

The ability to erase text is just as valuable and necessary as the ability to create text. Deleting text is part of writing text, part of thinking and rethinking, and part of self-editing. Writing. Deleting. Rewriting. Redeleting. That's how it goes!

Both creating and destroying text are accomplished by using the keyboard. The majority of keys are used to create text. Only two keys delete text: Backspace and Delete. How these keys work, and how much of your text they can delete, depends on how the keys are used, as described in this section.

Deleting single characters

Use the Backspace and Delete keys by themselves to delete single characters:

- **Backspace key:** Deletes the character to the left of the insertion pointer
- **Delete key:** Deletes the character to the right of the insertion pointer

In the following example, the insertion pointer is "flashing" (okay, it *would* be flashing on a computer screen) between the *z* and the *e* in *dozens.* Pressing the Backspace key deletes the *z;* pressing the Delete key deletes the *e:*

```
Duane made doz|ens of
delightful things in his
woodshop yet still managed to
retain all his fingers.
```

The touchscreen keyboard features only the Backspace key, which, ironically, supports the universal symbol

for the Delete key. Touching this key backs up and
erases. There's no Delete key equivalent on the touchscreen keyboard to delete the character to the right
of the insertion pointer.

> ✔ After you delete a character, any text to the
>   right or below the character shuffles over to fill
>   the void.

> ✔ You can press and hold Backspace or Delete to
>   continuously "machine-gun-delete" characters.
>   Release the key to halt such wanton destruction.

Deleting a word

To gobble up an entire word, add the Ctrl key to the
Backspace or Delete key's destructive power:

> ✔ **Ctrl+Backspace** deletes the word in front (to
>   the left) of the insertion pointer, which puts the
>   cursor at the end of the preceding word (or
>   paragraph).

> ✔ **Ctrl+Delete** deletes the word behind (to the
>   right) of the insertion pointer, which puts the
>   cursor at the beginning of the next word.

These keyboard shortcuts work best when the insertion pointer is at the start or end of a word. When
you're in the middle of the word, the commands
delete only from that middle point to the start or
end of the word.

After deleting the text, Word neatly wraps up the
remaining text, snuggling it together in a grammati-
cally proper way; deleting a word doesn't leave a
"hole" in your text.

Deleting more than a word

Word lacks keyboard-specific commands to delete more than a word or character of text. Larger chunks of your document can be deleted, swiftly and effectively. It's just that those ways are not that obvious.

A line of text is merely a line across the page (not really a grammatical issue). The easiest way to delete a line of text is to use the mouse:

1. **Move the mouse into the left margin of your document.**

   You know you've found the sweet spot when the mouse pointer changes into a northeast arrow.

2. **Point the mouse pointer arrow at the line of text you want to obliterate.**

3. **Click the mouse.**

   The line of text is highlighted, or *selected*.

4. **Press the Delete key to send that line into oblivion.**

A sentence is a grammatical thing. You know: Start with a capital letter and end with a period, a question mark, or an exclamation point. You probably mastered this concept in grammar school, which is why they call it grammar school anyway. Making a sentence go bye-bye is cinchy:

1. **Hover the mouse over the offending sentence.**

2. **Press and hold the Ctrl key and click the mouse.**

   The sentence is selected.

3. **Press the Delete key.**

   Oomph! It's gone.

A paragraph is one or more sentences, or a heading, ending with a press of the Enter key. Here's the fastest way to delete a full paragraph:

1. **Point the mouse at the paragraph.**
2. **Click the mouse button thrice (3 times).**
3. **Press the Delete key.**

 If clicking thrice befuddles you, move the mouse pointer into the left margin, next to the offending paragraph. When the mouse pointer changes to a northeasterly pointing arrow, click twice to select the entire paragraph.

A page of text is just that — all the text from where the page starts to where the page ends. It's a physical thing. Pages are a formatting issue, not something Word deals with directly, with regard to editing. Even so, to delete a page, mind these steps:

1. **Press Ctrl+G to summon the Go To tab in the Find and Replace dialog box.**
2. **Choose Page from the Go to What list.**
3. **Type the number of the page you want to delete.**
4. **Click the Go To button and then click the Close button.**

   The insertion pointer is positioned at the top of the page you chose in Step 3.
5. **Press the F8 key to enter a special selection mode in Word (see details in Chapter 3).**
6. **Press Ctrl+PgDn (the Page Down key) to select the entire page.**
7. **Press the Delete key to delete the page.**

Word lets you delete any old odd-size chunk of text anywhere in your document. The key is to mark that text as a block. After the block is marked, you can press the Delete key to zap it to Kingdom Come. Refer to Chapter 3 for more information on blocks of text.

Split and Join Paragraphs

For some people, a paragraph in a word processor is a strange thing. It's basically a chunk of text. Like most things that come in chunks — cheese, meat, large men named Floyd — it's often necessary to split or combine them. Well, maybe not for Floyd.

Making two paragraphs from one

 To split a single paragraph in twain, locate the point where you want it to break — say, between two sentences. Move the insertion pointer to that location and then press the Enter key. Word splits the paragraph in two; the text above the insertion pointer becomes its own paragraph, and the text following it then becomes the next paragraph.

Depending on how the paragraph was torn asunder, you may need to delete an extra space at the beginning of the second paragraph or at the end of the first paragraph.

Making one paragraph from two

To join two paragraphs and turn them into one, you delete the Enter character between the paragraphs. To do that, move the insertion pointer to the start of the second paragraph and then press the Backspace key. Removing the Enter character joins two paragraphs.

Depending on how neatly the paragraphs were joined, you may need to add a space between the sentences at the spot where the paragraphs were glued together.

The Soft and Hard Returns

Pressing the Enter key in Word ends a paragraph. It's officially known as typing a *hard return.* Yes, it's *return* even though the key is known as Enter on a PC. Don't blame me for this odd nomenclature. I only write the books — not the programs.

The problem with the hard return is that it adds a bit of "air" after a paragraph, which can be a good thing. Those times when you don't want air, when you need to put lines of text close together, you use a soft return.

The *soft return,* or *line break,* is used primarily in titles and headings; when you have a long title and need to split it up between two lines, you press Shift+Enter to insert the soft return. For example, type this line:

```
Enjoying the Ballet
```

Press Shift+Enter. A new line starts. Continue typing:

```
A Guide for Husbands and Boyfriends
```

The soft return keeps the title text together (in the same paragraph), but on separate lines.

 You should also use the soft return when typing an address, either on an envelope or in a letter. Press Shift+Enter after typing each of these lines:

```
Mr. President
1600 Pennsylvania Ave.
Washington, DC 20500
```

If you try typing the same text and press Enter instead, you see more space between the lines, which isn't what you want. Nope, that soft return can sure come in handy.

Undo Mistakes with Undo Haste

The Undo command undoes anything you do in Word, which includes formatting text, moving blocks, typing and deleting text, formatting — the whole enchilada. You have two handy ways to unleash the Undo command:

- Press Ctrl+Z.

- Click the Undo command button on the Quick Access Toolbar.

> I prefer using the Ctrl+Z key combination, but an advantage of the Undo command button is that it sports a drop-down menu that helps you review the past several things you've done, or that can be undone.

- Word's Undo command is handy, but don't use it as an excuse to be sloppy!

- Regrettably, you cannot pick and choose from the Undo command button's drop-down menu; you can merely undo multiple instances of things all at one time.

- The Undo command works sporadically sometimes. Before this happens, Word warns you. For example, you may see a message such as "There is not enough memory to undo this operation, Continue?" Proceed at your own peril.

✔ The Undo command doesn't work when there's
  nothing to undo or if something simply cannot
  be undone. For example, you cannot undo a
  save-to-disk operation.

✔ To undo an Undo, choose Redo. See the next
  section.

Undoing the Undo command with Redo

If you undo something and — whoops! — you didn't
mean to, you must use the Redo command to set
things back to the way they were. For example, you
may type some text and then use Undo to "untype"
the text. You can use the Redo command to restore
the typing. You have two choices:

✔ Press Ctrl+Y.

✔ Click the Redo command button on the Quick
  Access Toolbar.

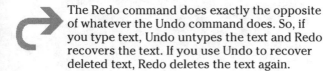

The Redo command does exactly the opposite
of whatever the Undo command does. So, if
you type text, Undo untypes the text and Redo
recovers the text. If you use Undo to recover
deleted text, Redo deletes the text again.

Using the Repeat command

When the Redo command has nothing left to
redo, it changes functions and becomes the
Repeat command. Its function is to repeat the
last thing you did in Word, whether it's typing
text, applying a format, or doing a variety of
other things.

Lamentably, you can't use the Repeat command to ease your typing chores. That's because it repeats only the last single character you typed. The keyboard shortcut for the Repeat command is Ctrl+Y, the same as the Redo command.

Chapter 5

Finding It, Replacing It, and Spelling It Write

- -

In This Chapter

▶ Finding text in your document, even if you can't type it

▶ Hunting down formatting codes

▶ Replacing found text with other text

▶ Fixing formatting with the Replace command

▶ Dealing with typos and spelling errors

▶ Correcting words automatically

▶ Checking AutoCorrect settings

- -

*L*ittle Bo Peep has lost her sheep. Too bad she
doesn't know about Word's Find and Replace
commands. She could find the misplaced ruminants
in a matter of nanoseconds. Not only that, she could
use search-and-replace to, say, replace all the sheep
with real estate. It's all cinchy after you understand
and use the various Find and Replace commands that
I cover in this chapter.

And did you know that there's no such thing as spelling in English? Spelling in English evolved over time.
Even the venerable Bard, William Shakespeare, spelled
his own name several different ways. It wasn't until

the notion of the "dictionary" appeared that spelling became more or less standardized. And Word tries its best to help apply the standards by including an on-the-fly and in-your-face spelling checker. This chapter describes how it works, when to use it, and how to disregard it.

Text Happily Found

Finding text is the domain of the Editing group, found on the far right end of the Home tab on Word's Ribbon interface. The Editing command button group may appear in its full glory, shown in Figure 5-1, or, when Word's window is too narrow, simply as an Editing button. When it's a button, you must click the button first to see the palette of commands.

Figure 5-1: The Editing group.

Finding a tidbit o' text

Word can quickly and graphically locate text in your document, from the smallest iota to the world's longest run-on sentence. Abide by these steps:

1. **On the Home tab, click the Find button in the Editing group or use the keyboard shortcut Ctrl+F to see the Navigation pane, illustrated in Figure 5-2.**

Search text

View page previews.

Clear search text.

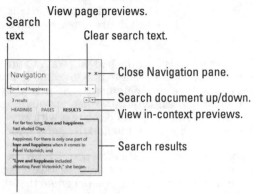

Close Navigation pane.

Search document up/down.

View in-context previews.

Search results

Click or touch a result to see that text in your document.

Figure 5-2. The Navigation pane helps you locate text.

2. **Type the text you want to find.**

   As you type, matching text is highlighted in the document. Depending on which tab is chosen in the Navigation pane, you see a summary of matching results beneath the text box.

3. **Click the up or down arrows (refer to Figure 5-2) to page through the search results until you find the exact chunk of text you want.**

   As you page, the document scrolls to find the next matching bit of text. Text is highlighted in your document, which makes visually searching easier.

4. **Close the Navigation pane when you're done hunting down text.**

When text can't be found, the Navigation pane tells you that it can't find the text. It uses the pronoun *we,* which I find disturbing.

 Be exact when typing the text you want to find. For example, if you want to find love and happiness, type **love and happiness** — no period or spaces or quotes. Type only the text you're looking for. And do not end the text with a period unless you want to find the period, too.

 If you're not sure whether the text is typed in uppercase or lowercase letters, use lowercase. If the text isn't found and you're *certain* that it's in there, check your spelling. If it's correct, try searching for a single word rather than two or more words or a sentence.

Scouring your document with Advanced Find

The Navigation pane is sweet, like the ideal prom date. But you don't really want the ideal prom date. No, you desire a date that you don't necessarily want to show Mom and Dad. In Word, the prom date you really want for finding text is the traditional Find dialog box, the one that lived in the neighborhood before the Navigation pane rolled into town.

To unleash the Advanced Find command, obey these steps:

1. **Ensure that your parents don't know what you're up to.**

2. **On the Ribbon's Home tab, click the menu arrow (a down-pointing triangle) next to the Find command button in the Editing group.**

3. **Choose Advanced Find to see the traditional Find dialog box (which I find more powerful and precise than the Navigation pane; Shhh!).**

4. **Click the More button.**

    Upon success, the Find and Replace dialog box grows taller, with a bunch of options and doodads showing at the bottom — its über-abilities — as illustrated in Figure 5-3.

> Options set for the Advanced Find command remain set until you turn them off. If you can't seem to locate text that you *know* is in your document, review the settings in the Advanced Find dialog box. Turn off the ones you no longer need.

Unveil Search Options.

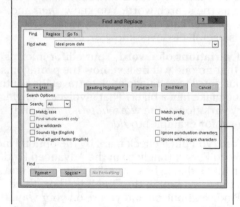

Set search   Search option über abilities.
direction.

Figure 5-3: The Advanced Find dialog box.

The following list explains how you can use the Advanced Find command:

- ✔ **To find an exact bit of text.** There's a difference between *Pat* and *pat*. One is a name, and the other is to lightly touch something. To use the Find command to find one and not the other, select the Match Case option under Search Options. That way, *Pat* matches only words that start with an uppercase *P* and have lowercase *at* in them.

- ✔ **To find a whole word.** Use the Find Whole Words Only option to look for words such as *elf* and *ogre* without also finding words like *shelf* and *progress*.

- ✔ **Find text that sounds like something else.** The Sounds Like (English) option allows you to search for *homonyms,* or words that sound the same as the search word. You know: *their* and *there,* or *deer* and *dear,* or *hear* and *here.* How this is useful, I'll never know.

- ✔ **Find variations of a word.** Your editor informs you that no one will believe how the protagonist in your novel uses a pogo stick to travel the South. So you make him a biker. That involves changing every variation of the word *hop* (*hopping* and *hopped,* for example) to *ride*.

  In Word, you put a check mark by the option Find All Word Forms (English) in the Advanced Find command's dialog box (refer to Figure 5-3) and type the word **hop** in the Find What box. Click the Find Next button and you're on your way.

- ✔ **Search this way or that.** Word normally searches from the insertion pointer's position to the end of a document and then back 'round the top again. You can override this stubbornness by placing your hand on the Find command's tiller in the Search drop-down list (refer to Figure 5-3).

You have the option to search Down (from the insertion pointer's location to the end of your document), Up (from the insertion pointer's location to the start of your document), or All (the entire document).

You can use keyboard shortcuts to search up or down. The Ctrl+PgDn key combination repeats the last search downward; the Ctrl+PgUp key combination repeats the most recent search upward.

Finding stuff you can't type

You can search for certain items in a document that you just cannot type at the keyboard. No, I'm not talking about nasty things — this isn't a censorship issue. Instead, I'm referring to items such as tabs, Enter keys (paragraphs), page breaks, graphics, and other, similar nontypeable things.

The techniques described in the list that follows use the Advanced Find dialog box, described in the earlier section, "Scouring your document with Advanced Find." Also refer to Figure 5-3.

✔ **Find special characters.** To hunt down untypeable characters in your document, click the Special button in the Advanced Find dialog box. Up pops a list of 22 items that Word can search for but that you would have a dickens of a time typing.

Choose an item from the list to search for that special character. When you do, a funky shorthand representation for that character (such as ^t for Tab) appears in the Find What box. Click the Find Next button to find that character.

There are probably only a half dozen of the special character items you'll eventually (if ever) use — including Any Character, Any Digit, and

Any Letter — which are special characters that can be used as wild cards for matching lots of stuff.

✔ **Find formatting.** In its most powerful superhero mode, the Find command can scour your document for formatting information. For example, if you want to find only those instances of the word *lie* in **boldface type**, you can do that.

Click the Format button in the Advanced Find dialog box to display a pop-up menu of Word's primary formatting commands. Choosing any item from that list displays a corresponding dialog box, from which you can choose the formatting attributes to search for.

If you want to search only for a format, leave the Find What text box blank. That way, you can search for formatting attributes without caring what the text reads. And, yes, you can search for more than one formatting attribute at a time. Just keep choosing format options from the Format button.

The Find command remembers your formatting options! The next time you want to search for plain text, click the No Formatting button. Doing so removes the formatting attributes and allows you to search for text in any format.

Replace Found Text

The Find command is good only for finding stuff. When you want to find something and replace it with something else, you use the Find and Replace command. This section describes the details.

Replacing one thing with another

Suppose that you may want to change all instances of *ungulates* in your document to *ruminants*. Here's how that's done:

1. **On the Home tab, click the Replace command button in the Editing group on the far right side of the Ribbon, or press Ctrl+H.**

   Choosing the Replace command button displays the Find and Replace dialog box, as shown in Figure 5-4.

Figure 5-4: The Replace tab of the Find and Replace dialog box.

2. **In the Find What box, type the text you want to find and press the Tab key when you're done typing.**

3. **In the Replace With box, type the text you want to use to replace the original text.**

4. **Click the Find Next button.**

   At this point, the Replace command works just like the Find command: Word scours your document for the text you typed in the Find What dialog box. When that text is found, you move on to Step 5; otherwise, the Replace command fails because there's nothing to replace.

5. **Click the Replace button.**

   Word replaces the found text, highlighted onscreen, with the text typed in the Replace With box.

   Word may find and replace your text in the middle of another word, such as *use* in *causes*. Oops! Click the More button and select the Find Whole Words Only option to prevent such a thing from happening.

6. **Continue replacing.**

   After you click the Replace button, Word immediately searches for the next instance of the text, at which point you repeat Step 5 until the entire document has been searched.

7. **Read the summary that's displayed in the dialog box that appears when the operation is complete.**

8. **Click the Close button.**

You're done! *But note:* The Replace command's dialog box also sports a More button, which can be used exactly as the More button for the Find command. See the section "Scouring your document with Advanced Find," earlier in this chapter.

If you don't type anything in the Replace With box, Word replaces your text with *nothing!* It's wanton destruction!

Speaking of wanton destruction, the Undo command restores your document to its preceding condition if you foul up the Replace operation. See Chapter 4 for more information.

Replacing it all at once

The steps in the previous section work well to find and replace tidbits of text around your document. But it can often be tedious to keep clicking that Replace button over and over. That's why the Replace command's dialog box sports the handy Replace All button.

The Replace All button directs the Replace command to find all instances of the Find What text and — without question — replace it with the Replace With text. To use this button, simply click the Replace All button in Step 5 in the preceding section. Then skip to Step 8.

 Be doubly certain that you made the proper settings in the Find and Replace dialog box before you click that Replace All button! You can still undo any mistakes, but for a large document, a lot of text can be found and replaced in a manner most merciless.

Finding and replacing formatting

Just as the Find command can search for text with specific formatting, you can use the Replace command to replace text and apply formatting or to replace one type of formatting with another. Needless to say, this process can be tricky: Not only do I recommend that you be familiar with Word's formatting commands, but you should also be well practiced in using the Find and Replace command.

Suppose that you want to replace all instances of underlined text with italic. (Underlined text reeks so much of typewriter, and that's just too 20th century for these modern times.) By replacing underline with italic, you're searching for one text format and replacing it with another; you're not even searching for text. So be careful. Do this:

1. **Press Ctrl+H to summon the Find and Replace dialog box.**

2. **Click the mouse in the Find What text box and press the Delete key to remove any text.**

3. **Click the More button, if necessary, to display the full dialog box.**

4. **Click the Format button and choose Font from the pop-up menu that appears.**

5. **In the resulting Find Font dialog box, choose the single underline graphic from the Underline style drop-down list, and then click the OK button.**

   Back in the Find and Replace dialog box, the text `Format: Underline` appears below the Find What box.

6. **Click the Replace With text box and press Backspace to delete that text.**

   To replace one format with another, such as underline with italic, be sure to leave the Find What and Replace With text boxes empty. That way, only the text formatting is replaced.

7. **Choose Font from the Format button's pop-up list.**

8. **In the Replace Font dialog box, choose (None) as the underline style.**

   This step is necessary because, otherwise, Word wouldn't remove the first style; it would merely add to that style. Likewise, text attributes such as Not Bold and Not Italic are found in the Replace Font dialog box.

9. **Choose Italic from the Font Style list, and then click OK to close the Replace Font dialog box.**

   Below the Replace With box, it should say `Format: Font: Italic, No underline`. That means Word will search for underlined text and replace it with italic text *and* remove the underline.

10. **Click the Replace All button.**

    Word scours your document and replaces any
    underlined text with italic.

11. **Click OK when the find-and-replace is done.**

As long as you set things up carefully, searching and
replacing text formatting is a quick and easy way to
spiff up a boring document.

Check Your Spelling

Spell checking in Word works the second you start
typing. Offending or unknown words are immediately
underlined with the red zigzag of shame. Word can
also be employed to scan the entire document, word
by word, for your attempts at mangling the English
language. Word can be trained to use the AutoCorrect
feature to automatically correct your common typos
and misspellings. This section describes the details.

Checking words as you type

Word has an internal library stocked with zillions of
words, all spelled correctly. Every time you type a word,
it's checked against that dictionary. When the word
isn't found, it's marked as suspect in your document.
The mark is a red zigzag underline. I'm sure you've
seen it.

My advice: Keep typing. Don't let the "red zigzag of a
failed elementary education" perturb you. Focus on
getting your thoughts up on the screen rather than on
stopping and fussing over inevitable typos.

When you're ready, say, during one of those inevitable
pauses that takes place as you write, go back and fix
your spelling errors. Here's what to do:

1. **Locate the misspelled word by looking for the red zigzag underline.**

2. **Right-click the misspelled word, and up pops a shortcut menu, as shown in Figure 5-5.**

Last night, she allowed me to tickle her fachy.

fancy

fanny

Ignore All

Add to Dictionary

Hyperlink...

New Comment

Figure 5-5: Deal with that typo.

3. **Choose from the list the word you intended to type.**

   In Figure 5-5, the word *fancy* fits the bill. Click that word and it's automatically inserted into your document, to replace the spurious word.

If the word you intended to type isn't on the list, don't fret. You may have to use a traditional dictionary (the paper kind) or take another stab at spelling the word phonetically and then correct it again.

Dealing with words incorrectly flagged as being misspelled

Occasionally, Word's spell checker bumps into a word it doesn't recognize, such as your last name or perhaps your city. Word dutifully casts doubt on the word, by underlining it with the notorious red zigzag. Yes, this case is one of those where the computer is wrong.

Two commands are on the spell checker's right-click menu (refer to Figure 5-5) to deal with those false negatives: Ignore All and Add to Dictionary.

✔ **Ignore All:** Select this command when the word is properly spelled and you don't want Word to keep flagging it as misspelled in the current document.

For example, your science fiction short story has a character named Zadlux. Word believes it to be a spelling error, but you (and all the people of the soon-to-be-conquered planet Drebulon) know better. After you choose the Ignore All command, all instances of the suspect word are cheerfully ignored, but only in that document.

✔ **Add to Dictionary:** This command adds words to Word's custom dictionary, which is a supplemental list of correctly spelled words that are used to proof a document.

For example, I once lived on Pilchuck Avenue, which Word thinks is a misspelling of the word *Paycheck.* If only. So, when I right-click the incorrectly flagged word, I choose the Add to Dictionary command. Presto — the word *Pilchuck* is added to Word's custom dictionary. I'll never have to spell-check that word again.

Word doesn't spell-check certain types of words — for example, words with numbers in them or words written in all capitals, which are usually abbreviations. For example, Pic6 is ignored because it has a 6 in it. The word *NYEP* is ignored because it's in all caps.

If the word looks correct but is red-wiggly-underlined anyway, it could be a repeated word. They're flagged as misspelled by Word, so you can choose to either delete the repeated word or just ignore it.

Undoing the Ignore All command

Choosing the Ignore All command means that all instances of a given misspelled word or typo are considered correctly spelled in your current document (but only in this document). This statement holds true even when you save that document and open it again later. So, if you make a mistake and would rather have the ignored word regarded once more, do this:

1. **Choose the Options command from the File tab's menu.**

2. **Choose Proofing on the left side of the Word Options window.**

3. **Click the Recheck Document button.**

   A warning dialog box appears, reminding you of what you're about to do.

4. **Click the Yes button.**

   Everything you've told Word to ignore while proofing your document is now ignored. It's the ignore-ignore command!

5. **Click the OK button to return to your document.**

By following these steps, you direct Word to un-ignore not only all previously ignored words but also any grammatical errors you've chosen to ignore. You have no way to undo this command.

Removing words from the custom dictionary

When you choose the Add to Dictionary command, the given word is placed into the custom dictionary. Recognizing that people may change their minds, Word allows you to edit its custom dictionary, to remove words you may have added accidentally. To remove unwanted words from the custom dictionary, follow these steps:

1. **Click the Word Options button on the File tab's menu.**

2. **From the left side of the Word Options window, choose Proofing.**

3. **Click the button labeled Custom Dictionaries to see the Custom Dictionaries dialog box.**

4. **Select the item RoamingCustom.dic (Default).**

5. **Click the button labeled Edit Word List.**

   You see a scrolling list of words you've added to the custom dictionary.

6. **Find and select the word you want to remove from the dictionary by clicking it once.**

7. **Click the Delete button.**

8. **Repeat Steps 6 and 7 if you want to remove more words.**

9. **Click the OK button when you're done editing the dictionary.**

AutoCorrect Your Common Typos

Some typos and spelling errors are never graced by the red zigzag. That's because Word quickly fixes hundreds of common typos and spelling errors on the fly. The AutoCorrect feature does it, and you have to be quick to see it.

Understanding AutoCorrect

There's nothing to using AutoCorrect; it happens automatically. In Word, try to type the word *mispell.* You can't! Word uses AutoCorrect and suddenly you see *misspell.*

Most commonly misspelled words can be found in AutoCorrect's repertoire: *acomodate, suposed, recieve,* and so on. Try a few. See whether you can baffle Word!

In addition to fixing spelling errors, AutoCorrect helps you enter special characters. For example, type **(C)** and AutoCorrect properly inserts the © copyright symbol. Ditto for **(TM)** for the trademark. Typing --> is translated into an arrow, and even :) becomes a happy face.

Beyond spelling, AutoCorrect fixes certain common punctuation. It automatically capitalizes the first letter of a sentence. AutoCorrect capitalizes *I* when you forget to, properly capitalizes the names of days, fixes the iNVERSE cAPS lOCK pROBLEM, plus other common typos.

Undoing an AutoCorrect correction

You can reverse AutoCorrect instant changes, but only when you're quick. The secret is to press Ctrl+Z (the Undo command) immediately after AutoCorrect makes its correction. The change is gone.

When AutoCorrect fixes a word, a blue rectangle appears under the first letter. That's your key to access AutoCorrect options and change the way AutoCorrect behaves: Point the mouse at the rectangle to see a button, which you can then click to see various AutoCorrect options, as shown in Figure 5-6.

Figure 5-6: Adjusting an AutoCorrection.

Here are your options:

✔ **Change Back to "*whatever*":** Undo the AutoCorrection.

✔ **Stop Automatically Correcting "*whatever*":** Remove the word from the AutoCorrect dictionary so that it's not corrected automatically again. (But it may still be flagged as incorrect by the spell checker.)

✔ **Control AutoCorrect Options:** Display the AutoCorrect dialog box, which is used to customize various AutoCorrect settings and to edit or create new entries in the AutoCorrect library.

Control Word's Spell-Check and AutoCorrect Options

All document-proofing options and settings are kept in one place, buried deep in Word's bosom. Here's how to get there:

1. **Click the File tab.**

2. **Choose Options from the File tab's menu.**

3. **In the Word Options window, choose Proofing from the left side.**

The right side of the window contains options and settings for document proofing. When you find yourself in this Proofing corner, you can change spell-check settings. To turn off on-the-fly spell checking, remove the check mark by the item Check Spelling As You Type.

You can also click the AutoCorrect Options button in the Word Options window to view the AutoCorrect dialog box and its slew of automatic word-correcting and typo-fixing options, as shown in Figure 5-7.

Figure 5-7: Oodles of AutoCorrect options.

Here are some things you can do:

- ✔ The AutoCorrect tab lists all problems that AutoCorrect fixes for you, plus common typo corrections. That's also where you can remove the AutoCorrect entries you detest.

- ✔ The AutoFormat tab also harbors those insidious options that automatically create bulleted lists and heading styles in Word; remove the appropriate check marks to disable those unwanted features.

- ✔ Also refer to the AutoFormat As You Type tab to kill off additional automatic numbering and bulleted list features in Word.

If you don't like how Word changes web page addresses in your document into real hyperlinks, remove the check mark by the option Internet and Network Paths with Hyperlinks on the AutoFormat tab.

When you're done working in the Word Options window, click the OK button to lock in whichever changes you've made.

Chapter 6

Formatting Characters and Paragraphs

● ●

In This Chapter

▶ Choosing a font and applying basic text formats

▶ Changing text size, color, and case

▶ Undoing text formatting

▶ Exploring the Font dialog box

▶ Finding paragraph-formatting commands

▶ Aligning paragraphs left, center, right, and full

▶ Changing spacing between lines and paragraphs

▶ Adding indentations

● ●

*J*ust as your body is composed of millions of cells,
documents are composed of thousands of characters. Like a cell, a *character* is the basic building block
of the document. Characters include letters, symbols,
and Aunt Eunice, who claims to talk with squirrels
and even knits sweaters for them.

The most basic element you can format in a document
is text — the letters, numbers, and characters you type.
You can format text to be bold, underlined, italicized,

little, or big or in different fonts or colors — all sorts of pretty and distracting attributes. Word gives you a magnificent amount of control over the appearance of your text. This chapter contains the details.

Word also lets you hang many attributes onto a paragraph, probably more than you realize. Beyond alignment and margins, there are ways to format spacing in and around a paragraph of text. There are also special formatting commands just for the first line of a paragraph. Then there's the agonizing subject of tabs, which is really a paragraph-formatting attribute, but too much of a nut for me to include in this chapter. So I cover only the essentials of paragraph formatting.

Text Formatting 101

You can change the format of your text in two ways:

- ✔ **Choose a text-formatting command first, and then type the text.** All the text you type is formatted as chosen.

- ✔ **Type the text first, and then select the text as a block and apply the formatting.** This technique works best when you're busy with a thought and need to return to format the text later.

You use both methods as you compose text in your document. Sometimes, it's easier to use a formatting command and type the text in that format. For example:

1. **Type this line:** The cake was

2. **Press Ctrl+I to activate** *italic text.*

3. **Type this word:** really
4. **Press Ctrl+I again, which turns off italic.**
5. **Continue typing:** salty.

The final sentence looks like this:

> The cake was *really* salty.

For more complex formatting, type the text first, go back, mark the text as a block, and then apply the formatting: Type the sentence **The cake was really salty**, and then double-click the word *really* to select it. Press Ctrl+I.

See Chapter 3 for more information on marking blocks of text.

Basic Text Formatting

Word stores some of the most common text-formatting commands on the Home tab, in the Font group, as shown in Figure 6-1. The command buttons in this group carry out most of the basic text formatting you use in Word. This section mulls over the possibilities.

The Font group can help you quickly determine which type of formatting is applied to your text. For example, in Figure 6-1, the text where the insertion pointer is blinking is formatted in the Calibri font. The number 11 tells you that the text is 11 points tall. If the B button were highlighted, you would also know that the text was formatted in bold. (These text formats are discussed throughout this section.)

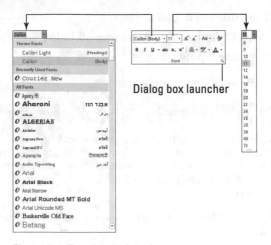

Dialog box launcher

Figure 6-1: Text-formatting gizmos.

When no font is displayed in the Font group (the listing is blank), it means that more than one font is being used in the selected block of text.

Changing the font

The most basic attribute of text is its *typeface,* or *font.* The font sets up the way your text looks — its overall text style. Although deciding on a proper font may be agonizing (and, indeed, many graphic artists are paid well to choose just the right font), the task of selecting a font in Word is quite easy. It generally goes like this:

1. **On the Home tab, in the Font group, click the down arrow to display the Font Face list.**

   A menu of font options appears, as shown on the left in Figure 6-1.

2. **Scroll to the font you want.**

The fonts in the All Fonts part of the list are displayed in alphabetical order as well as in context (as they appear when printed).

> You can quickly scroll to a specific part of the menu by typing the first letter of the font you need, such as T for Times New Roman.

3. Click to select a font.

> You can also use the Font menu to preview the look of fonts. Scroll through the list to see which fonts are available and how they may look. As you move the mouse over a font, any selected text in your document is visually updated to show how that text would look in that font. The text isn't changed until you select the new font.

Graphic designers prefer to use two fonts in a document — one for the text and one for headings and titles. Word is configured this way as well. The font you see with `Body` after its name is the current text, or *body,* font. The font marked as `Headings` is used for headings.

Applying character formats

The Font group lists some of the most common character formats. They're applied in addition to the font. In fact, they enhance the font. Use them as you see fit:

To make text bold, press Ctrl+B or click the Bold command button. Use **bold** to make text stand out on a page — for titles and captions or when you're uncontrollably angry.

To make text italic, press Ctrl+I or click the Italic command button. *Italic* has replaced underlining as the preferred text-emphasis format. Italicized text is light and wispy, poetic and free.

Underline text by pressing Ctrl+U or clicking the Underline command button. You can click the down arrow next to the Underline command button to choose from a variety of underline styles or set an underline color. <u>Underline</u> is what they use at the DMV when they're feeling saucy.

Strike through text by clicking the ~~Strikethrough~~ command button. (There's no keyboard shortcut for this one.) I don't know why strikethrough text made it to the Font group. If I were king of Microsoft, I would have put small caps up there instead. But who am I? Strikethrough is commonly used in legal documents, when you mean to say something but then ~~change your mind~~ and think of something better to say.

Make text subscript by pressing Ctrl+= (equal sign) or clicking the Subscript command button. Subscript text appears below the baseline, such as the 2 in H_2O. Again, I'm puzzled about how this formatting command ranks up there with bold and italic. I suppose that there's a lot of subscripting going on somewhere.

Make text superscript by pressing Ctrl+Shift+= (equal sign) or clicking the Superscript command button. Superscript text appears above the line, such as the 10 in 2^{10}.

More text formats are available in Word, such as small caps, outline, and shadow. You can access them from the Font dialog box. Refer to the section "Fun with the Font Dialog Box," later in this chapter.

Basic character formatting affects only selected text or any new text you type.

✔ To turn off a text attribute, use the command
again. For example, press Ctrl+I to type in *italic*.
Then press Ctrl+I again to return to normal text.

✔ You can mix and match character formats. For
example, press Ctrl+B and then Ctrl+I to apply
bold and italic text. You press Ctrl+B and Ctrl+I,
or the command buttons, to turn off these attributes again.

The best way to use superscript or subscript is
to write text first. Then go back, mark as a block
the text you want to superscript or subscript,
and *then* use these commands. So 42 becomes 4^2
and CnH2n+1OH becomes $C_nH_{2n+1}OH$. Otherwise,
when you apply super- or subscript, the text you
modify tends to be rather teensy and hard to
edit. Better to write it first and then format.

Using less-common
character attributes

Here are a few more text attributes — call them second-
string players. You may not use these as often as bold
or italic, but Word makes them available to you just
as well:

✔ To switch to **all caps** text, press Ctrl+Shift+A. This
is a text format, not applied by pressing the Shift
or Caps Lock key. In fact, like other formats, it
can be removed. (Also see the later section,
"Change Text Case.")

✔ To set **double-underlined** text, press
Ctrl+Shift+D. <u>This text is double-underlined.</u>

✔ To produce **small caps**, press Ctrl+Shift+K. Small
caps formatting is ideal for headings. I use it for
character names when I write a script or play:

BILL. That's a clever way to smuggle a live grenade into prison.

✔ To **underline words only**, and not the spaces between words, press Ctrl+Shift+W. <u>Word</u> <u>underlining</u> <u>looks</u> <u>like</u> <u>this</u>.

You create hidden text by pressing Ctrl+Shift+H. Hidden text is good for what it says — hiding text in a document. Of course, you don't see the text onscreen, either. To show hidden text, click the Show/Hide command button (in the Paragraph group on the Home tab) as described in Chapter 2, in the section about dealing with spots and clutter in the text. The hidden text shows up in the document with a dotted underline.

Text Transcending Teeny to Titanic

In Word, you can choose the size of your text, from indecipherably small to monstrously huge. Of course, more common is the subtle text-size adjustment; rare is the student who hasn't fudged the length of a term paper by inching up the text size a notch or two.

Understanding points

Word (and Windows) deals with text size as measured in *points*. It's a typesetting term. One point is equal to $\frac{1}{72}$ inch. Don't bother memorizing it. Instead, here are some point pointers:

✔ The bigger the point size, the larger the text.

✔ Most printed text is either 10 or 12 points tall.

✔ Headings are typically 14 to 24 points tall.

✔ Most fonts can be sized from 1 point to 1,638 points. Point sizes smaller than 6 are generally too small for a human to read.

✔ Seventy-two points is equal (roughly) to 1-inch-high letters.

The point size of text is a measure from the bottom of the descender to the top of the ascender — from the bottom of the lowercase *p* to the top of the capital *E,* for example. So the typical letter in a font is smaller than its given font size. In fact, depending on the font design, text formatted at the same size but with different fonts *(typefaces)* may not appear to be the same size. It's just one of those typesetting oddities that causes regular computer users to start binge drinking.

Setting the text size

Text size is set in the Font group on the Home tab. Immediately to the right of the Font box is the Size box. Clicking the down arrow displays a list of font sizes for your text, as shown on the right in Figure 6-1.

The Size menu lists only common text sizes. To set the text size to a value that isn't listed or to a specific value, type the value in the box. For example, to set the font size to 11.5, click in the Size box and type **11.5**.

You can preview the new text size by pointing the mouse at an item on the Size menu. The word under the insertion pointer, or a selected block of text, is updated on the screen to reflect the new size. Click to choose a size or press Esc to cancel.

Nudging text size

Sometimes, choosing text size is like hanging a picture: To make the picture level on the wall, you have to nudge it just a little this way or that. Word has similar tools for nudging the text size larger or smaller, two of which are found in the Font group.

To increase the font size, click the **Grow Font** command button or press Ctrl+Shift+>. The Grow Font command nudges the font size up to the next value as listed on the Size menu (refer to Figure 6-1). So if the text is 12 points, the Grow Font command increases its size to 14 points.

To decrease the font size, click the **Shrink Font** command button or press Ctrl+Shift+<. The Shrink Font command works in the opposite direction of the Grow Font command, by reducing the text size to the next-lower value as displayed on the Size menu.

When you want to increase or decrease the font size by smaller increments, use these shortcut keys: Ctrl+] makes text one point size larger; Ctrl+[makes text one point size smaller.

More Colorful Characters

Adding color to your text doesn't make your writing more colorful. All it does is make you wish that you had more color ink when it's time to print your document. Regardless, you can splash around color on your text, and there's no need to place a drop cloth in the document's footer.

Text color is applied by clicking the **Font Color** command button. The bar below the *A* on the Font Color command button indicates which color is applied to text.

To change the color, you must click the menu arrow to the right of the Font Color command button. A color menu appears, which I don't show in this book because it's not in color and the image would bore you. Even so, as you move the mouse pointer over various colors on the menu, selected text in your document is updated to reflect that color. When you find the color you like, click it. That color then becomes the new text color associated with the Font Color command button.

✔ Select the More Colors item from the Font Color menu to display the special Colors dialog box. Use the dialog box to craft your own, custom colors.

✔ The *Automatic* color refers to the color that's defined for the text style you're using.

✔ The Font Color command affects only the text color, not the background.

✔ Be careful with the colors you use! Faint colors can make text extremely difficult to read. If you want to hide text in your document, use the Hidden text attribute, described elsewhere in this chapter.

Colored text prints in color only when a color printer is available and readily stocked with color ink.

Be careful not to confuse the Font Color command button with the Text Highlight Color command button, to its left. Text highlighting is a text attribute, but it's best used for document markup.

Change Text Case

Believe it or not, upper- and lowercase have something to do with a font. Back in the old days of mechanical type, a font came in a case, like a briefcase. The top part of the case, the upper case, held the capital letters. The bottom part of the case held the noncapital letters. So, in a way, changing the case of text is a font-formatting trick.

 To change the case of text in Word, use the **Change Case** command button in the Font group. Choosing this button displays a menu of options, each showing a different way to capitalize words in a sentence. Select the text you want to change, and then choose the proper item from the Change Case command button. Your text is modified to match the menu item that's selected.

You can also use the Shift+F3 command to change the case of selected text. But this keyboard shortcut cycles between only three of the menu options shown in the figure: ALL CAPS, lowercase, and Capitalize Each Word.

Remove Character Formatting

So many Word formatting commands are available that it's possible for your text to look more like a pile of formatting remnants than anything that's readable in any human language. Word understands this problem, so it created the Clear Formatting command to let you peel away all formats from your text, just like you peel the skin from a banana:

 To blow away formatting from a block of selected text or the text the insertion pointer is on or future text you type, use the **Clear Formatting** command button in the Font group. The keyboard shortcut for this command is Ctrl+spacebar.

The Clear Formatting command removes any formats you've applied to the text: font, size, text attributes (bold or italic), color, and so on.

✔ The Clear Formatting command removes the ALL CAPS text format but doesn't change the case of text you created by using Shift, Caps Lock, or the Change Case command in Word.

✔ Another key combination for Ctrl+spacebar is Ctrl+Shift+Z. Remember that Ctrl+Z is the Undo command. To undo formatting, all you do is add the Shift key, which may make sense — well, heck, if any of this makes sense.

Fun with the Font Dialog Box

Word has a place where all your font-formatting delights are kept in a neatly organized fashion. It's the Font dialog box, as shown in Figure 6-2.

Figure 6-2: The neatly organized Font dialog box.

To summon the Font dialog box, click the Dialog Box Launcher button in the lower-right corner of the Font group (refer to Figure 6-1) or press the Ctrl+D keyboard shortcut.

The Font dialog box contains *all* the commands for formatting text, including quite a few that didn't find their way into the Font group on the Ribbon. As with all text formatting, the commands you choose in the Font dialog box affect any new text you type or any selected text in your document.

When you're done setting up your font stuff, click the OK button. Or click Cancel if you're just visiting.

 The best benefit of the Font dialog box is its Preview window, at the bottom. This window shows you exactly how your choices affect text in your document.

✔ Click the Text Effects button in the Font dialog box to access festive attributes such as Shadow, Outline, Emboss, and Engrave. They're useful for titles and headings.

✔ You can use the Advanced tab in the Font dialog box to set options for changing the size and position of text on a line.

 The Set As Default button in the Font dialog box is used to change the font that Word uses for a new document. If you prefer to use a specific font for all your documents, choose the font (plus other text attributes) in the Font dialog box, and then click the Set As Default button. In the dialog box that appears, choose the option All Documents Based on the Normal Template, and then click the OK button. Afterward, all documents start with the font options you selected.

How to Format a Paragraph

Question: What is a paragraph?

Answer: A mechanical gizmo that lets you draw pears.

Real Answer: A sentence or collection of sentences expressing a thought.

Word Formatting Answer: A chunk of text that ends when you press the Enter key. So, as long as you type a single character, word, or sentence and then press Enter, you have a paragraph in Word.

You can format a paragraph in several ways:

- ✔ With the insertion pointer in a paragraph, use a formatting command to format that paragraph. This trick works because all paragraph-formatting commands affect the paragraph in which the insertion pointer is blinking.

- ✔ Use a paragraph-formatting command, and then type a new paragraph in that format.

- ✔ Use the formatting command on a block of selected paragraphs to format them all at once. To format all paragraphs in a document, press Ctrl+A to select all text in the document.

Some folks like to see the Enter key symbol (¶) in their documents, visually marking the end of every paragraph. You can do this in Word by following these steps:

1. **Click the File tab.**

2. **Choose the Options command from the File screen to open the Word Options dialog box.**

3. **Click Display.**

4. **Place a check mark by Paragraph Marks.**

5. **Click OK.**

Now, every time you press the Enter key, the ¶ symbol appears at the end of the paragraph.

Where the Paragraph Formatting Commands Lurk

In a vain effort to confuse you, Word has placed popular paragraph-formatting commands in not one but *two* locations on the Ribbon. The first place to look is in the Paragraph group, found on the Home tab. The second place is in the Paragraph group found on the Page Layout tab. Both groups are illustrated in Figure 6-3.

Dialog box launcher   Dialog box launcher

Home Tab   Page Layout Tab
Paragraph Group   Paragraph Group

Figure 6-3: Paragraph groups.

But wait! There's more.

The Paragraph dialog box, shown in Figure 6-4, can be conjured up by clicking the dialog box launcher button in either of the Paragraph groups (refer to Figure 6-3). In it, you find some finer controls that the command buttons on the Ribbon just don't offer.

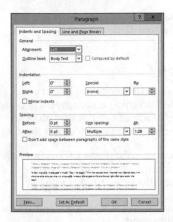

Figure 6-4: The Paragraph dialog box.

Click the Cancel button or press the Esc key to dismiss the Paragraph dialog box.

The obnoxious keyboard shortcut to summon the Paragraph dialog box is Alt, H, P, G. Don't mock it! If you can remember the keyboard shortcut, it saves you time.

The Mini toolbar, which shows up after you select text, also contains a smattering of paragraph-formatting buttons.

Paragraph Justification and Alignment

Paragraph alignment has nothing to do with politics, and justification has nothing to do with the right or wrong of how paragraphs are formatted. Instead, both terms refer to how the left and right edges of the paragraph look on a page. The four options are Left, Center, Right, and Fully Justified.

Line up on the left!

Much to the pleasure of southpaws the English-speaking world over, left-aligning a paragraph is considered normal: The left side of the paragraph is all even and tidy, and the right side is jagged, not lined up.

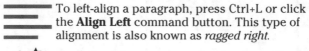 To left-align a paragraph, press Ctrl+L or click the **Align Left** command button. This type of alignment is also known as *ragged right*.

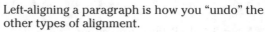 Left-aligning a paragraph is how you "undo" the other types of alignment.

Everyone center!

Centering a paragraph places each line in that paragraph in the middle of the page, with an equal amount of space to the line's right or left.

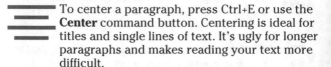 To center a paragraph, press Ctrl+E or use the **Center** command button. Centering is ideal for titles and single lines of text. It's ugly for longer paragraphs and makes reading your text more difficult.

Line up on the right!

A *right-aligned* paragraph has its right margin nice and even. The left margin, however, is jagged. When do you use this type of formatting? I have no idea, but it sure feels funky typing a right-aligned paragraph.

To flush text along the right side of the page, press Ctrl+R or click the **Align Right** command button. This type of alignment is also known as *ragged left* or *flush right*.

Line up on both sides!

Lining up both sides of a paragraph is *full justification:* Both the left and right sides of a paragraph are neat and tidy, flush with the margins. Word makes each side of the paragraph line up by inserting tiny slivers of extra space between words in a paragraph.

 To give your paragraph full justification, press Ctrl+J or click the Justify command button. Fully justified paragraph formatting is often used in newspapers and magazines, which makes the narrow columns of text easier to read.

Make Room Before, After, or Inside Paragraphs

Word lets you add "air" to the space before or after or in the middle of your paragraphs. In the middle of the paragraph, you have line spacing. Before and after the paragraph comes paragraph spacing. Figure 6-5 shows you where the spacing can be found. The following sections describe how to control that spacing.

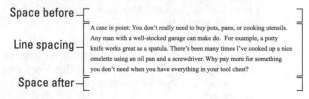

Space before ⎤
Line spacing ⎥ A case in point: You don't really need to buy pots, pans, or cooking utensils. Any man with a well-stocked garage can make do. For example, a putty knife works great as a spatula. There's been many times I've cooked up a nice omelette using an oil pan and a screwdriver. Why pay more for something you don't need when you have everything in your tool chest?
Space after ⎦

Figure 6-5: Spacing in and around a paragraph.

Setting the line spacing

Changing the line spacing inserts extra space between *all* lines of text in a paragraph. Because Word adds the space *below* each line of text in the paragraph, the last line in the paragraph will also have a little extra space after it.

 The **Line Spacing** command button is found in the Home tab's Paragraph group. Click this button to view a menu listing common line-spacing values. Choose a new line-spacing value from the menu to change the line spacing for the current paragraph or all paragraphs selected as a block.

✔ Word sets line spacing at 1.08 as its standard, or *default*. Supposedly, that extra .08 lines of text makes text more readable than using single spacing, or 1.0.

✔ To double-space your text, choose the value 2.0 from the Line Spacing command button menu. This setting formats the paragraph with one blank line below each line of text. To triple-space, choose the value 3.0, which makes one line of text appear with two blank lines below it.

✔ Ah, the keyboard shortcuts! To single-space, press Ctrl+1. To double-space, press Ctrl+2. To use 1½-space lines, press Ctrl+5.

Yes, Ctrl+5 applies 1½-line spacing, not 5-line spacing. Use the 5 key in the typewriter area of the computer keyboard. Pressing the 5 key on the numeric keypad activates the Select All command.

✔ There's no such thing as having no line spacing. If you want to "remove" fancy line spacing, select some text and press Ctrl+1 for single spacing.

When you want text to stack up one line atop another line, such as when typing a return address, use the *soft return* at the end of a line: Press Shift+Enter. See the section in Chapter 4 about soft and hard returns.

Setting specific line-spacing options

For persnickety line spacing, you summon the Paragraph dialog box (refer to Figure 6-4). In the Spacing area of the dialog box, use the Line Spacing drop-down list to set various line-spacing values: Single, 1.5, and Double, as found on the Line Spacing command button menu.

Some options in the Line Spacing drop-down list require you to also use the At box to sate your specific line-spacing desires. Values set in the At box indicate line spacing, as described in this list:

- ✔ **At least:** The line spacing is set to the specified value, which Word treats as a minimum value. Word can disobey that value and add more space whenever necessary to make room for larger type, different fonts, or graphics on the same line of text.

- ✔ **Exactly:** Word uses the specified line spacing and doesn't adjust the spacing to accommodate larger text or graphics.

- ✔ **Multiple:** This option is used to enter line-spacing values other than those specified in the Line Spacing drop-down list.

Click the OK button to confirm your settings and close the Paragraph dialog box.

Making space between paragraphs

It's a silly thing to do: Press Enter twice to end a paragraph. People say that they need the extra space between the paragraphs for readability. That's true, but what they don't realize is that Word can add that space automatically. The secret is to use the Before and After paragraph formatting commands — commands that have nothing to do with losing weight.

To add room after a paragraph, use the After command. It's found in the Page Layout tab's Paragraph group (refer to Figure 6-3). To add room before a paragraph, use the Before command, also found on the Page Layout tab's Paragraph group. Both commands are also found in the Paragraph dialog box, in the Spacing area (refer to Figure 6-4).

- The space you add before or after a paragraph becomes part of its format. Most of the time, space is added after a paragraph.

- You can add space before a paragraph, for example, to further separate text from a document heading or subhead.

- The values used in the After or Before boxes are *points,* not inches or potrzebies. Points are also used in Word to set text size.

- Adding space before or after a paragraph is a great way to spread out a list of bullet points or numbered steps without affecting the line spacing within the bullet points or steps.

Paragraph Indentation

Do you suffer from the shame of manual paragraph indenting? It's a hidden secret. Yes, even though computers enjoy doing tasks automatically, too many

Word users still begin a paragraph of text by pressing the Tab key. It's ugly, but it's a topic that must be discussed.

Word can indent your paragraphs for you: left side, right side, both sides, or maybe just the first line. It can even outdent the first line, which is truly something to behold. This section discusses various paragraph-indenting and -outdenting options.

Indenting the first line of a paragraph

To have Word automatically indent the first line of every paragraph you type, heed these steps:

1. **Conjure up the Paragraph dialog box by clicking the dialog box launcher button in the Paragraph group on either the Home or Page Layout tab.**

2. **In the Indentation area, locate the Special drop-down list.**

3. **Select First Line from the list.**

4. **Enter an amount in the By box (optional).**

   Unless you've messed with the settings, the box should automatically say 0.5", which means that Word automatically indents the first line of every paragraph a half inch — one tab stop.

5. **Click OK and the selected block, or the current paragraph, automatically gets an indented first line.**

To remove the first-line indent from a paragraph, repeat these steps and select (none) from the drop-down list in Step 3. Then click the OK button.

Making a hanging indent (an outdent)

A *hanging indent* isn't in imminent peril, nor can it affect the outcome of an election. Instead, it's a paragraph in which the first line sticks out to the left and the rest of the paragraph is indented — it's a preferred way to present paragraph lists — like this:

Snore putty: It works every time. Just apply a little snore putty to your partner's mouth and nostrils. In just moments, that rattling din is gone and you're back to sleeping comfortably.

To create such a beast, position the insertion pointer in the paragraph you want to hang and indent. Press Ctrl+T, the Hanging Indent keyboard shortcut. As a bonus, every time you press Ctrl+T, the paragraph is indented by another half inch.

Because you probably won't remember Ctrl+T all the time (who could?), paragraphs can also be hanged and indented in the Paragraph dialog box. Follow the steps from the preceding section, but in Step 3 choose Hanging from the drop-down list.

 To undo a hanging indent, press Ctrl+Shift+T. That's the unhang key combination, and it puts the paragraph's neck back in shape.

Indenting a whole paragraph

Just as you can indent the first line of a paragraph, you can indent every line of a paragraph, by moving the paragraph's left margin over to the right a notch, just like Mr. Bunny: Hop, hop, hop. This technique is popular for typing block quotes or *nested* paragraphs.

To indent a paragraph one tab stop from the left, click the **Increase Indent** command button in the Home tab's Paragraph group or press Ctrl+M.

 To unindent an indented paragraph, click the **Decrease Indent** command button in the Home tab's Paragraph group or press Ctrl+Shift+M.

Each time you use the Increase Indent command, the paragraph's left edge hops over one tab stop (typically, one half-inch). To undo this and shuffle the paragraph back to the left, use the Decrease Indent command.

When you want to get specific, you can set the left and right indents for a paragraph by using the Page Layout tab's Paragraph group or the Paragraph dialog box. (Refer to Figure 6-4.) The Left item sets the indentation of the paragraph's left edge. The Right item sets the indentation of the paragraph's right edge.

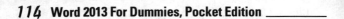

Chapter 7

Saving and Publishing Your Documents

. . . .

In This Chapter

▶ Creating, opening, and saving documents

▶ Inserting one document inside another

▶ Closing a document

▶ Retrieving a lost document

▶ Getting the printer ready to print

▶ Previewing and printing your document

▶ Making a document compatible for sharing

▶ Attaching documents to e-mail

. . . .

I like the word *document*. It's elegant. It's much better than saying "a file" or "that thing I created with my word processor." A document could include everything from a shopping list to a note excusing little Jimmy's absence.

Regardless of size or importance, it's called a *document*. It's the goal of your using Word. You'll create new documents, conjure up old documents to work on them again, save documents, and close documents. This chapter covers document basics.

A long time ago, the final step in document creation was printing your masterpiece to show the world. The process was called simply *printing* because you could do little else with the document. Times have changed.

Today, the final step in the word processing saga is *publishing*. Publishing a Word document means printing, but it also includes other electronic ways to share your document: Send it by e-mail, post it to a website, stick it on a blog somewhere, or engage in other electronic adventures. It's all publishing.

Behold! A New Document

All documents begin life plucked from the electronic ether. The empty document is presented on the screen like a blank sheet of paper, ready for you to compose your thoughts. You can summon a new document from the Word Start screen by clicking the Blank Document item. Or, after you've started your Word session, you can bring forth a new document by obeying these steps:

1. **Click the File tab.**
2. **Choose the New command from the left side of the resulting file screen window.**
3. **In the New screen that appears (with a slew of confusing options), click the Blank Document item.**

    The Word window returns to normal and you see a blank page, ready for typing.

You can repeat these steps as often as you need new documents; Word lets you work with several documents at a time.

Ah, the shortcut: Press Ctrl+N to quickly summon a new, blank document in Word.

Save Your Stuff!

It doesn't matter whether you've written a masterpiece or are jotting down notes for tonight's PTA meeting, the most important thing you can do to a document is *save it.* Saving creates a permanent copy of your document, encoding your text as a file on the computer's storage system. That way, you can work on the document again, publish it electronically, or have a copy ready in case the power goes *poof.* All these tasks require saving.

Saving a document the first time

Don't think that you have to wait until you finish a document to save it. In fact, you should save almost immediately — as soon as you have a few sentences or paragraphs. Save! Save! Save!

To save a document for the first time, follow these steps:

1. **Click the File tab and choose the Save As command.**

   The Save As screen appears, similar to the one shown in Figure 7-1. This screen is an intermediate step before the traditional Save As dialog box. It allows you to choose a location for your document, either locally or on the Internet.

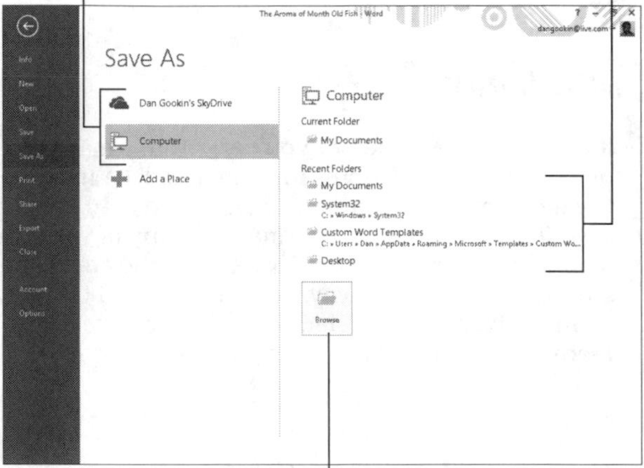

Locations to save your document   Choose a recent folder.

Summon the traditional Save As dialog box.

Figure 7-1: The Save As screen.

2. **Choose a location for the document; choose the Computer item to create and save the document on your own computer, which is what I recommend.**

3. **Click the Browse button, or choose an item from the Recent Folders list.**

4. **In the Save As dialog box that appears, type a name for your document in the File Name box.**

   Word automatically selects the first line or first several words of your document as a filename and puts it in the Save As dialog box. If that's okay, you can move to Step 5. Otherwise, type a descriptive name in the File Name box.

5. **Work the options in the Save As dialog box (optional).**

6. **Click the Save button.**

   The file is now safely stored in the computer's storage system. Your clue that the file has been successfully saved is that the name you gave it (the filename) now appears on the document's title bar, at the top center of the Word window.

At this point, you can keep working. As you work, continue to save, as outlined in the upcoming section "Saving or updating a document."

 From the And-Now-He-Tells-Us Department, you don't really need to work through Step 1 the first time you save a document. Instead, you can click the Save button on the Quick Access Toolbar. Because the document hasn't yet been saved, the Save As screen appears automatically.

Dealing with document-save errors

Saving a document involves working with both Word and the Windows operating system. This process doubles the chances of something going wrong, so it's high time for an error message. A potential message you may see is The file *whatever* already exists.

You have three choices:

- ✔ **Replace Existing File:** Nope.
- ✔ **Save Changes with a Different Name:** Yep.
- ✔ **Merge Changes into Existing File:** Nope.

After choosing the middle option, type a different file name in the Save As dialog box.

Another common problem occurs when a message that's displayed reads something like this:

```
The file name is not valid
```

That's Word's less-than-cheerful way of telling you that the filename contains a boo-boo character. To be safe, stick to letters, numbers, and spaces when you're naming a file.

Saving or updating a document

Every so often as you continue to work on your document, you should save again. That way, any changes you've made since the last time you saved are remembered and recorded on the computer's storage system permanently. To resave a document that has already been saved to disk, click the File tab and choose the Save command from the File screen. You get no feedback, and the Save As dialog box doesn't show up. That's because you already gave the file a name; the Save command merely updates the existing file.

Open a Document

Saving a document means nothing unless you have a way to retrieve it. You have several ways to *open* a document that was previously saved as a file. This section mulls the possibilities.

Using the Open command

Open is the standard computer command used to fetch a document that already exists on the computer's storage system. You use Open to hunt down documents, and the document is then displayed in Word's window as though it has always been there.

To grab a document you already worked on — to *open* it — follow these steps:

1. **Click the File tab to display the File screen.**

2. **Choose the Open command.**

   The shortcut key to get to the Open screen is Ctrl+O.

3. **In the Open screen that appears (as shown in Figure 7-2), choose a location where the document may lurk.**

   Your choices are Recent Documents, the SkyDrive, or your computer.

Places to look for a document   Choose a recent document.

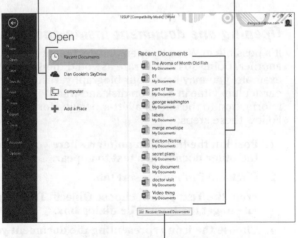

Rescue an unsaved document.

Figure 7-2: The Open screen.

> If you can find your document in the Recent
> Documents list, click it. The document opens on
> the screen. Congratulations — you're done. If you
> don't see your document, you have to continue
> hunting for it on the SkyDrive or your computer.

4. **Choose a recent folder from the list or click the
   Browse button when the recent folders displayed do not please you.**

5. **In the Open dialog box, click to highlight the
   file you want to open.**

6. **Click the Open button, and Word opens the
   highlighted file and slaps it down on the screen.**

After the document is open, you can edit it, look at it,
print it, or do whatever you want.

Opening one document inside another

It's possible in Word to open one document inside of
another. Doing so isn't as rare as you'd think. For
example, you may have your biography, résumé, or
curriculum vitae in a file on disk and want to add that
information to the end of a letter begging for a job.
Follow these steps:

1. **Position the insertion pointer where you want
   the other document's text to appear.**

2. **Click the Ribbon's Insert tab.**

3. **From the Text group, choose Object⇨Text from
   File to get the Insert File dialog box.**

4. **Choose the icon representing the document you
   want to insert.**

   You can also use the gadgets and gizmos in the
   dialog box to locate a file in another folder or on
   another disk drive or even on someone else's
   computer on the network. Such power!

5. **Click the Insert button.**

The document you selected is inserted into the current document, just as though you had typed (and formatted) the whole thing, right there with your stubby little fingers. The resulting combined document still has the same name as the first document; the document you inserted remains unchanged.

Close a Document

When you're done writing a document, you need to do the electronic equivalent of putting it away. That electronic equivalent is the Close command: Choose the Close command from the File screen, or use the handy Ctrl+W keyboard shortcut.

If you haven't saved your document recently, Word prompts you to save before you close; click the Save button and the document is saved. (If it hasn't yet been saved — shame on you! — you see the Save As dialog box, as described earlier in this chapter.)

You don't have to choose the Close command. You can click the X (Close) button in the upper-right corner of the Word window, which is almost the same thing: You're prompted to save your document if it needs saving. But when you click the X button, you also quit Word.

Recover a Draft

Computers crash. Users forget to save in a pinch. Or perhaps another type of disaster has befallen your unsaved Word document. When the planets are properly aligned and the word processing gods are smiling, it's possible to recover those lost documents, the ones that Word calls *drafts*. Here's how:

1. **Click the File tab to view the File screen.**

2. **Choose the Open command.**

3. **Choose Recent Documents.**

   You see the list of recent documents (refer to Figure 7-2). When unsaved drafts are available, you see a button at the bottom of the list: Recover Unsaved Documents.

4. **Click the Recover Unsaved Documents button.**

5. **In the Open dialog box that appears, choose from the list a document to recover.**

   The document may have an unusual name, especially when it has never been saved.

6. **Click the Open button to open and recover the document.**

The document you recover might not be the one you wanted it to be. If so, try again and choose another document. You might also find that the document doesn't contain all the text you typed or thought would be there. You can't do anything about it, other than *remember to save everything* in the first place!

Your Document on Paper

Getting it down on paper has been the goal of writers ever since paper was invented. The word processor, the best writing tool ever invented, is also the first writing tool to utterly avoid paper. You can change that situation, however, by using the most traditional method to publish your document: Print it. You use a printer, either attached directly to your computer or available on a network, to create a *hard copy* of your document.

Preparing the printer

Before you print a document, I recommend following these steps to ensure that the printer is ready to print:

1. **Make sure that your printer is plugged in and properly connected to your computer.**

2. **Ensure that your laser printer has plenty of toner or that your ink printer's cartridges are brimming with ink.**

3. **Check the printer for paper.**

4. **Turn on the printer.**

5. **Your printer must be *online* or *selected* before you can print.**

   This is weird: Some printers can be on but not ready to print. The power is on, but unless the printer is online or selected, it ignores the computer. To force these types of printers to listen to the computer, you must press the Online, Ready, or Select (or similar) button.

Previewing before printing

Before you print, preview the look of the final document. Yeah, even though your document is supposed to look the same on the screen as it does on paper, you may still see surprises: missing page numbers, blank pages, screwy headers, and other jaw-dropping blunders, for example.

Fortunately, a print preview of your document appears as part of the Print screen, as shown in Figure 7-3.

Back button/ Return to document.

Print document.   Pages text box

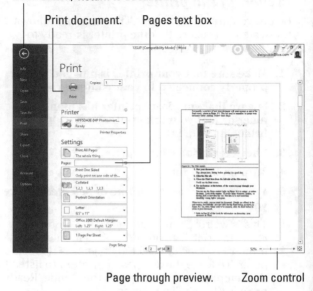

Page through preview.   Zoom control

Figure 7-3: The Print screen.

You only need to remember to peruse your document before printing it. Follow these steps:

1. **Save your document.**

2. **Click the File tab.**

3. **Chose the Print item from the left side of the File screen.**

4. **In the Print screen that appears, use the buttons at the bottom of the screen to page through your document.**

   You can use the Zoom control (refer to Figure 7-3) to enlarge or reduce the image. Look at the margins. If you're using footnotes, headers, or footers, look at how they lay out. The idea is to spot anything that's dreadfully wrong *before* you print.

When you're ready, you can print the document. Details are offered in the next section, but basically you click the big Print button, as shown in Figure 7-3. Or when things need to be repaired, click the Back button to return to your document.

Printing the whole document

Printing the document is easy to do:

1. **Make sure that the printer is on and ready to print, and that your document is saved.**

2. **Click the File tab.**

3. **Choose the Print command from the File tab's window.**

4. **In the Print screen that appears, click the big Print button.**

   The keyboard shortcut to display the Print screen is Ctrl+P.

   The Print screen closes, and the document spews forth from the printer. Printing may take some time — a *long* time. Fortunately, you can continue working while the document prints.

If nothing prints, don't use the Print command again! If you don't see an error message, everything will probably print, eventually. The computer prints one copy of your document for every Print command you incant. If the printer is just being slow and you impatiently click the Print button ten times, you print ten copies of your document.

Printing a specific page

Follow these steps to print only one page of your document:

1. **Move the insertion pointer so that it's sitting somewhere on the page you want to print.**

   Check the page number on the status bar to ensure that you're on the right page.

2. **Choose the Print command from the File screen, or press Ctrl+P.**

3. **Click the button beneath the Settings heading and choose Print Current Page from the menu.**

4. **Click the Print button.**

The single page prints with all the formatting you applied, including footnotes and page numbers and everything else, just as though you plucked that page from a complete printing of the entire document.

Printing a range of pages

Word enables you to print a range of pages, odd pages, even pages, or a hodgepodge combination of random pages from within your document. To print a range or group of pages, summon the Print screen, as described earlier in this chapter.

Your key to printing a hodgepodge of pages is to use the Pages text box (refer to Figure 7-3). Here are some suggestions for what to type in that text box:

To print pages 3 through 5, for example, type **3-5**.

To print pages 1 through 7, type **1-7**.

To print pages 2 and 6, type **2,6**.

To print page 3, pages 5 through 9, pages 15

through 17, and page 19 (boy, that coffee went
everywhere, didn't it?), type **3,5-9,15-17,19**.

Click the big Print button when you're ready to print.
Only the pages you specify churn from the printer.

Printing odd and even pages

To print all odd pages, click the Print All Pages button
on the Print screen. Choose the command Only Print
Odd Pages from the menu. To print only even pages,
choose the command Only Print Even Pages. Click the
big Print button, and only those pages you've chosen
print.

Printing a block

After you mark a block of text onscreen, you can beg
the Print command to print only that block. Here's how:

1. **Mark the block of text you want to print.**

2. **Summon the Print screen.**

3. **From the button beneath the Settings heading,
   choose the item Print Selection, which is available only when a block is selected in your
   document.**

4. **Click the Print button.**

Printing more than one copy of something

Imagine how silly it would be to send your résumé to
a company but add that you need your résumé returned
because you have only one copy. Word can easily
print multiple copies of any document. Here's how:

1. **Press Ctrl+P on the keyboard to summon the Print screen.**

2. **Enter the number of copies in the Copies text box.**

3. **Click the big Print button to print your copies.**

Under normal circumstances, Word prints each copy of the document one after the other. This process is known as *collating*. However, if you're printing seven copies of a document and you want Word to print seven copies of page 1 and then seven copies of page 2 (and so on), choose the option Uncollated from the Collated menu button, found under the Settings heading on the Print screen.

Choosing another printer

Your computer can have more than one printer attached. Even small offices and home offices have computers networked and sharing printers. Choose a different printer on the Print screen by clicking the button beneath the Printer heading. A list of available printers appears; simply choose a printer from the list. Make other settings in the window as well, and then click the big Print button. Your document prints on the chosen printer.

Electronic Publishing

Mr. Bunny likes to live in the forest. It's his home. The forest is full of trees and friendly critters. It's also home to predators who would love to eat Mr. Bunny, but that's not my point. My point is that you can do your part to help save Mr. Bunny's home by publishing your documents electronically. Keep this statement in mind: It's not always necessary to print your documents.

Preparing a document for sharing

Lots of interesting things can be put into your Word document that you don't want published. These items include comments, revision marks, hidden text, and other items useful to you or your collaborators, which would mess up a document you share with others. The solution is to use Word's Check for Issues tool, like this:

1. **Ensure that your document is finished, finalized, and saved.**

2. **Click the File tab and click the word *Info* (if the Info area is not highlighted already).**

3. **Click the Check for Issues button.**

4. **Choose Inspect Document from the Check for Issues button menu.**

5. **Click the Inspect button in the resulting Document Inspector window.**

    After a few moments, the Document Inspector window shows up again, listing any issues with your document. The issues shown are explained, which allows you to cancel out of the Document Inspector to fix individual items.

6. **Click the Remove All button next to any issues you want to clear up.**

    Remember that this step is entirely optional. Now that you know what the issues are, you can always click the Close button and return to your document to manually inspect them.

7. **Click the Close button, or click Reinspect to give your document another once-over.**

8. **Click the Back button to return to your document.**

Sending a document by e-mail

E-mailing your Word document is a snap — as long as you're using Microsoft Outlook as your e-mail program. This opening statement also implies that your organization uses an "Exchange Server." If that's you, great — you can follow these steps to e-mail your document:

1. **Save your document one more time.**

2. **Click the File tab and choose the Share command.**

3. **Choose the E-Mail item found under the Share heading.**

4. **Click the Send As Attachment button.**

   At this point, Outlook takes over and you compose your e-mail message. When you send the message, your Word document is sent along as well.

If you don't use Outlook (and I don't blame you), you can always send a Word document just as you send any e-mail file attachment. The key is to save the document *and* remember its filename and location so that you can find it later. To attach a Word document to an e-mail message by using just about any e-mail program, follow these general steps:

1. **Compose your e-mail message as you normally do.**

2. **Use the Attach command to find the Word document and attach it to the message.**

3. **Send the message.**

Chapter 8

The Ten Commandments of Word

• •

1 admit that I look nothing like Charlton Heston. Though I'm only guessing, I probably look nothing like Moses, either. Still, I feel compelled to return from Mount Sinai with some basic codes for word processing. I call them my Ten Commandments of Word.

Thou Shalt Remember to Save Thy Work

Save! Save! Save! Always save your stuff. Whenever your mind wanders, have your fingers dart over to the Ctrl+S keyboard shortcut. Savest thy work.

Thou Shalt Not Use More Than One Space

Generally speaking, you should never find more than one space anywhere in a Word document. The appearance of two or more spaces in a row is a desperate cry for a tab. Use single spaces to separate words and sentences. Use tabs to indent or to align text on a tab stop.

Thou Shalt Not Press Enter at the End of a Line

Word automatically wraps text. As you type and your text approaches the right margin, the words automatically advance to the next line. Therefore, there's no need to press the Enter key, unless you want to start a new paragraph. When you don't want to start a new paragraph but you need to start a new line, such as when typing a return address, press Shift+Enter, the *soft* return command.

Thou Shalt Not Neglect Thy Keyboard

Word is not Windows. Windows is a graphical operating system. Graphics means using the mouse. So, although you can get lots done with the mouse, some things in Word are done faster by using the keyboard.

For example, stab the Ctrl+S key combo to quickly save a document. Pressing Ctrl+P to print works better than fumbling for the mouse, as does Ctrl+O to open a document. You don't have to know all the keyboard commands, but remembering a few helps.

Thou Shalt Not Manually Number Thy Pages

Word has an automatic page-numbering command. Word can not only automatically number your pages, but it also lets you place the page number just about anywhere on the page and in a variety of fun and interesting formats. Just click the Insert tab and choose the Page Number command button from the

Header & Footer group. Then choose where to place
the page numbers and the page numbering style from
the resulting sequential menus.

Thou Shalt Not Press the Enter Key to Start a New Page

When you need to start text at the top of a new page,
you use the *manual page-break* command. Its keyboard shortcut is Ctrl+Enter. That's the best and most
proper way to start a new page. The worst way to
start a new page is to brazenly press the Enter key a
couple of dozen times. Although the result may look
okay, this strategy doesn't guarantee anything; as you
continue to edit your document, the page break
moves back and forth and ends up looking butt-ugly.

Thou Shalt Not Forget Thy Undo Command

Just about anything that happens in Word can be
undone by choosing the Undo command from the
Quick Access toolbar or pressing the popular and
common keyboard shortcut Ctrl+Z.

Honor Thy Printer

The biggest printing problem anyone has is telling
Word to print something when the printer isn't on.
Verify that your printer is on, healthy, and ready to
print before you tell Word to print something.

Never (or at least try not to) continue trying the
Print command when a document doesn't print.

Word tries to print once every time you use the Print command. Somewhere and sometime, those documents will print, unless you do something to prevent it.

Thou Shalt Have Multiple Document Windows Before Thee

In Word, as in most Windows applications, you can work on more than one document at a time. In fact, you can have as many document windows open as you can stand (or until the computer runs out of memory). Word even lets you view a single document in multiple windows.

You don't have to close one document to open and view another document. You don't have to quit Word to run another program, either. In Windows, you can run multiple programs; so don't quit Word when you plan to start it again in just a little while.

Neglecteth Not Windows

Word is not Windows. Word is an application, designed for productivity. Windows is a computer operating system, designed to control a computer and to drive human beings crazy. These two different computer programs work together.

Windows is used to help keep *files* (the documents you create in Word) organized. You cannot do that in Word by itself. Therefore, verily I say unto you, don't feel that just because you're using Word, you can utterly skip out on Windows. You need them both in order to control your computer system.